The Great Push • Patrick MacGill

Publisher's Note

The book descriptions we ask booksellers to display prominently warn that the book may have numerous typos, missing text, images and indexes.

We scanned this book using character recognition software that includes an automated spell check. Our software is 99 percent accurate if the book is in good condition. However, we do understand that even one percent can be a very annoying number of typos! And sometimes all or part of a page is missing from our copy of a book. Or the paper may be so discolored from age that you can no longer read the type. Please accept our sincere apologies.

After we re-typeset and design a book, the page numbers change so the old index and table of contents no longer work. Therefore, we often remove them.

We would like to manually proof read and fix the typos and indexes, manually scan and add any illustrations, and track down another copy of the book to add any missing text. But our books sell so few copies, you would have to pay up to a thousand dollars for the book as a result.

Therefore, whenever possible, we let our customers download a free copy of the original typo-free scanned book. Simply enter the barcode number from the back cover of the paperback in the Free Book form at www.general-books.net. You may also qualify for a free trial membership in our book club to download up to four books for free. Simply enter the barcode number from the back cover onto the membership form on the same page. The book club entitles you to select from more than a million books at no additional charge. Simply enter the title or subject onto the search form to find the books.

If you have any questions, could you please be so kind as to consult our Frequently Asked Questions page at www.general-books.net/faqs.cfm? You are also welcome to contact us there.

General Books LLC®, Memp 2012. ISBN: 9781150901140.

❧ ❧ ❧ ❧ ❧ ❧ ❧

INTRODUCTION THE justice of the cause which endeavours to achieve its object by the murdering and maiming of mankind is apt to be doubted by a man who has come through a bayonet charge. The dead lying on the fields seem to ask, "Why has this been done to us? Why have you done it, brothers? What purpose has it served?" The battleline is a secret world, a world of curses. The guilty secrecy of war is shrouded in lies, and shielded by bloodstained swords; to know it you must be one of those who wage it, a party to dark and mysterious orgies of carnage. War is the purge of repleted kingdoms, needing a close place for its operations. I have tried in this book to give, as far as I am allowed, an account of an attack in which I took part. Practically the whole book was written in the scene of action, and the chapter dealing with our night at Les Brebis, prior to the Big Push, was written in the trench between midnight . -.and dawn of S'jptepiber 25th; the concluding chapter in the hospital at Versailles two days after I had been wounded at Loos.

Patrick Macgiix. THE GREAT PUSH
CHAPTER I IN THE ADVANCE TRENCHES

Now when we take the cobbled road
We often took before,
Our thoughts are with the hearty lads
　Who tread that way no more.

Oh! boys upon the level fields, If you could call to mind
The wine of Cafe Pierre le Blanc
　You wouldn't stay behind.
　　✓

But when we leave the trench at night, And stagger neath our load,
Grey, silent ghosts as light as air
　Come with us down the road.
　And when we sit us down to drink
You sit beside us too,
And drink at Cafe Pierre le Blanc
　As once you used to do.

THE Company marched from the village moon, corners, ...ghtly amidst the stars in the east, and under it, behind the German lines, a burning mine threw a flame, salmon pink and wreathed in smoke, into the air. Our Company was sadly thinned now, it had cast off many—so many of its men at Cuinchy, Givenchy, and Vermelles. At each of these places there are graves of the London Irish boys who have been killed in action.
We marched through a world of slag heaps and chimney stacks, the moonlight flowing down the sides of the former like mist, the smoke stood up from the latter straight as the chimneys themselves. The whirr of machinery in the mine could be heard, and the creaking wagon wheels on an adjoining railway spoke out in a low, monotonous clank the half strangled message of labour.

Our way lay up the hill, at the top we came into full view of the night of battle, the bursting shells up by Souchez, the flash of rifles by the village of Vermelles, the long white searchlights near Lens, and the star-shells, red, green and electric-white, rioting in a splendid blaze of colour over the decay, death and pity of the firing line. We could hear the dull thud of shells bursting in the fields and the sharp explosion they made amidst the masonry of deserted homes; you feel glad that the homes are deserted, and you hope that if any soldiers are billeted there they are in the safe protection of the cellars.

The road by which we marched was lined with houses all in various stages of collapse, some with merely a few tiles shot out of the roofs, others levelled to the ground. Some of the buildings were still peopled; at one home a woman was putting up the shutters and we could see some children drinking coffee from little tin mugs inside near the door; the garret of the house was blown in, the rafters stuck up over the tiles like long, accusing fingers, charging all who passed by with the mischief which had happened. The cats were crooning love songs on the roofs, and stray dogs slunk from the roadway as we approached. In the villages, with the natives gone and the laughter dead, there are always to be found stray dogs and love-making cats. The cats raise their primordial, instinctive yowl in villages raked with artillery fire, and poor lone dogs often cry at night to the moon, and their plaint is full of longing.

We marched down the reserve slope of the hill in silence. At the end of the road was the village; our firing trench fringed the outer row of houses. Two months before an impudent red chimney stack stood high in air here; but humbled now, it had fallen upon itself, and its own bricks lay still as sandbags at its base, a forgotten ghost with blurred outlines, it brooded, a stricken giant.

The long road down the hill was a tedious, deceptive way; it took a deal of marching to make the village. Bill Teake growled. "One would think the place was tied to a string," he grumbled, "and some one pullin' it away!"

We were going to dig a sap out from the front trench towards the German line; we drew our spades and shovels for the work from the Engineers' store at the rear and made our way into the labyrinth of trenches. Men were at their posts on the fire positions, their Balaclava helmets resting on their ears, their bayonets gleaming bright in the moonshine, their hands close to their rifle barrels. Sleepers lay stretched out on the banquette with their overcoats over their heads and bodies. Out on the front the Engineers had already taped out the night's work; our battalion had to dig some two hundred and fifty yards of trench 3 ft. wide and 6 ft. deep before dawn, and the work had to be performed with all possible dispatch. Rumour spoke of thrilling days ahead; and men spoke of a big push which was shortly to take place. Between the lines there are no slackers; the safety of a man so often depends upon the dexterous handling of his spade; the deeper a man digs, the better is his shelter from bullet and bomb; the spade is the key to safety.

The men set to work eagerly, one picked up the earth with a spade and a mate shovelled the loose stuff out over the meadow. The grass, very long now and tapering tall as the props that held the web of wire entanglements in air, shook gently backwards and forwards as the slight breezes caught it. The night was wonderfully calm and peaceful; it seemed as if heaven and earth held no threat for the men who delved in the alleys of war.

Out ahead lay the German trenches. I could discern their line of sandbags winding over the meadows and losing itself for a moment when it disappeared behind the ruins of a farm-house —a favourite resort of the enemy snipers, until our artillery blew the place to atoms. Silent and full of mystery as it lay there in the moonlight, the place had a strange fascination for me. How interesting it would be to go out there beyond our most advanced outpost and have a peep at the place all by myself. Being a stretcher-bearer there was no necessity for me to dig; my work began when my mates ceased their labours and fell wounded.

Out in front of me lay a line of barbed wire entanglements.

"Our wire?" I asked the Engineer.

"No—the Germans'," he answered.

I noticed a path through it, and I took my way to the other side. Behind me I could hear the thud of picks and the sharp, rasping sound of shovels digging into the earth, and now and again the whispered words of command passing from lip to lip. The long grass impeded my movements, tripping me as I walked, and lurking shellholes caught me twice by the foot and flung me to the ground. Twenty yards out from the wire I noticed in front of me something moving on the ground, wiggling, as I thought, towards the enemy's line. I threw myself flat and watched. There was no mistaking it now; it was a man, belly flat on the ground, moving off from our lines. Being a non-combatant I had no rifle, no weapon to defend myself with if attacked. I wriggled back a few yards, then got to my feet, recrossed the line of wires and found a company-sergeant-major speaking to an officer.

"There's somebody out there lying on the ground," I said. "A man moving off towards the German trenches."

The three of us went off together and approached the figure on the ground, which had hardly changed its position since I last saw it. It was dressed in khaki, the dark barrel of a rifle stretched out in front. I saw stripes on a khaki sleeve.
...

"One of a covering-party?" asked the sergeantmajor.

"That's right," came the answer from the grass, and a white face looked up at us.

"Quiet?" asked the S.-M.

"Nothing doing," said the voice from the ground. "It's cold lying here, though. We've been out for four hours."

"I did not think that the covering-party was so far out," said the officer, and the two men returned to their company.

I sat in the long grass with the watcher; he was the sergeant in command of the covering party.

"Are your party out digging?" he asked.

"Yes, out behind us," I answered. "Is the covering-party a large one?"

"About fifty of us," said the sergeant. "They've all got orders to shoot on sight when they see anything suspicious. Do you hear the Germans at work out there?"

I listened; from the right front came the sound of hammering.

"They're putting up barbed wire entanglements and digging a sap," said the sergeant. "Both sides are working and none are fighting. I must have another smoke," said the sergeant.

"But it's dangerous to strike a light here," I said.

"Not in this way," said the sergeant, drawing a cigarette and a patent flint tinder-lighter from his pocket. Over a hole newly dug in the earth, as if with a bayonet, the sergeant leant, lit the cigarette in its little dug-out, hiding the glow with his hand.

"Do you smoke?" he asked.

"Yes, I smoke," and the man gave me a cigarette.

It was so very quiet lying there. The

grasses nodded together, whispering to one another. To speak of the grasses whispering during the day is merely a sweet idea; but God! they do whisper at night. The ancients called the winds the Unseen Multitude; the grasses are long, tapering fingers laid on the lips of the winds. "Hush!" the night whispers. "Hush!" breathes the world. The grasses touch your ears, saying sleepily, "Hush! be quiet!"

At the end of half an hour I ventured to go nearer the German lines. The sergeant told me to be careful and not to go too close to the enemy's trenches or working parties. "And mind your own covering-party when you're coming in," said the sergeant. "They may slip you a bullet or two if you're unlucky."

Absurd silvery shadows chased one another up and down the entanglement props. In front, behind the German lines, I could hear sounds of railway wagons being shunted, and the clank of rails being unloaded. The enemy's transports were busy; they clattered along the roads, and now and again the neighing of horses came to my ears. On my right a working party was out; the clank of hammers filled the air. The Germans were strengthening their wire entanglements; the barbs stuck out, I could see them in front of me, waiting to rip our men if ever we dared to charge. I had a feeling of horror for a moment. Then, having one more look round, I went back, got through the line of outposts, and came up to our working party, which was deep in the earth already. Shovels and picks were rising and falling, and long lines of black clay bulked up on either side of the trench.

I took off my coat, got hold of a mate's idle shovel, and began to work.

"That my shovel?" said Bill Teake.

"Yes, I'm going to do a little," I answered. "It would never do much lying on the slope."

"I suppose it wouldn't," he answered. "Will you keep it goin' for a spell?"

"I'll do a little bit with it," I answered. "You've got to go to the back of the trenches if you're wanting to smoke."

"That's where I'm goin'," Bill replied. "'Ave yer got any matches?"

I handed him a box and bent to my work. It was quite easy to make headway; the clay was crisp and brittle, and the pick went in easily, making very little sound. M'Crone, one of our section, was working three paces ahead, shattering a square foot of earth at every blow of his instrument.

"It's very quiet here," he said. "I suppose they won't fire on us, having their own party out. By Jove, I'm sweating at this."

"When does the shift come to an end?" I asked.

"At dawn," came the reply. He rubbed the perspiration from his brow as he spoke. "The nights are growing longer," he, said, "and it will soon be winter again. It *will* be cold then."

As he spoke we heard the sound of rifle firing out by the German wires. Half a dozen shots were fired, then followed a long moment of silent suspense.

"There's something doing," said Pryor, leaning on his pick. "I wonder what it is."

Five minutes afterwards a sergeant and two men came in from listening patrol and reported to our officer.

"We've just encountered a strong German patrol between the lines," said the sergeant. "We exchanged shots with them and then withdrew. We have no casualties, but the Germans have one man out of action, shot through the stomach."

"How do you know it went through his stomach?" asked the officer.

"In this way," said the sergeant. "When we fired one of the Germans (we were quite close to them) put his hands across his stomach and fell to the ground yellin' 'Mein Gutt! Mein Gutt!'"

"So it did get 'im in the guts then," said Bill Teake, when he heard of the incident.

"You fool!" exclaimed Pryor. "It was 'My God' that the German said."

"But Pat 'as just told me that the German said 'Mine Gut,'" Bill protested.

"Well 'Mein Gott' (the Germans pronounce 'Gott' like 'Gutt' on a dark night) is the same as 'My God,' " said Pryor.

"Well, any'ow, that's just wot the Allymongs would say," Bill muttered. "It's just like them to call God Almighty nick names."

When dawn showed pale yellow in a cold sky, and stars were fading in the west, we packed up and took our way out and marched back to Nouex-les-Mines, there to rest for a day or two.

CHAPTER II OUT FROM NOUEX-LES-MINES

Every soldier to his trade—
Trigger sure and bayonet keen—
But we go forth to use a spade
Marching out from Nouex-les-Minea,

AS I was sitting in the Cafe Pierre le Blanc helping Bill Teake, my Cockney mate, to finish a bottle of vin rouge, a snubnosed soldier with thin lips who sat at a table opposite leant towards me and asked:

"Are you MacGill, the feller that writes?"

"Yes," I answered.

"Thought I twigged yer from the photo of yer phiz in the papers," said the man with the snub nose, as he turned to his mates who were illustrating a previous fight in lines of beer representing trenches on the table.

"See!" he said to them, "I knew 'im the moment I clapped my eyes on 'im."

"Hold your tongue," one of the men, a gingerheaded fellow, who had his trigger finger deep in beer, made answer. Then the dripping finger rose slowly and was placed carefully on the table.

"This," said Carrots, "is Richebourg, this drop of beer is the German trench, and these are our lines. Our regiment crossed at this point and made for this one, but somehow or another we missed our objective. Just another drop of beer and I'll show you where we got to; it was— Blimey! where's that bloomin' beer? 'Oo the 'ell 1 Oh! it's Gilhooley!"

I had never seen Gilhooley before, but I had often heard talk of him. Gilhooley was an Irishman and fought in an English regiment; he was notorious for his mad escapades, his dare-devil pranks, and his wild fearlessness. Now he was opposite to me, drinking a mate's beer, big, broadshouldered, ungainly Gilhooley.

The first impression the sight of him gave me was one of almost irresistible strength; I felt that if he caught a man around the waist with his hand he could, if he wished it, squeeze him to death. He was clumsily built, but an air of placid confidence in his own strength gave his figure a certain grace of its own. His eyes glowed brightly under heavy brows, his jowl thrust forward aggressively seemed to challenge all upon whom he fixed his gaze. It looked as if vast passions hidden in the man were thirsting to break free and rout everything. Gilhooley was a dangerous man to cross. Report had it that he was a bomber, and a master in this branch of warfare. Stories were told about him how he went over to the German trenches near Vermelles at dusk every day for a fortnight, and on each visit flung half a dozen bombs into the enemy's midst. Then he sauntered back to his own lines and reported to an officer, saying, "By Jasus! I go them out of it!"

Once, when a German sniper potting at our trenches in Vermelles picked off a few of our men, an exasperated English subaltern gripped a Webley revolver and clambered over the parapet.

"I'm going to stop that damned sniper," said the young officer. "I'm going to earn the V.C. Who's coming along with me?"

"I'm with you," said Gilhooley, scrambling lazily out into the open with a couple of pet bombs in his hand. "By Jasus! we'll get him out of it!"

The two men went forward for about twenty yards, when the officer fell with a bullet through his head. Gilhooley turned round and called back, "Any other officer wantin' to earn the V.C.?"

There was no reply: Gilhooley sauntered back, waited in the trench till dusk, when he went across to the sniper's abode with a bomb and "got him out of it."

A calamity occurred a few days later. The irrepressible Irishman was fooling with a bomb in the trench when it fell and exploded. Two soldiers were wounded, and Gilhooley went off to the Hospital at X. with a metal reminder of his discrepancy wedged in the soft of his thigh. There he saw Colonel Z., or "Up-you-go-and-thebest-of-luck," as Colonel Z. is known to the rank and file of the B.E.F.

The hospital at X. is a comfortable place, and the men are in no hurry to leave there for the trenches; but when Colonel Z. pronounces them fit they must hasten to the fighting line again.

Four men accompanied Gilhooley when he was considered fit for further fight. The five appeared before the Colonel.

"How do you feel?" the Colonel asked the first man.

"Not well at all," was the answer. "I can't eat 'ardly nuffink."

"That's the sort of man required up there," Colonel Z. answered. "So up you go and the best of luck."

"How far can you see?" the Colonel asked the next man, who had complained that his eyesight was bad.

"Only about fifty yards," was the answer.

"Your regiment is in trenches barely twentyfive yards from those of the enemy," the Colonel told him. "So up you go, and the best of luck."

"Off you go and find the man who wounded you," the third soldier was told; the fourth man confessed that he had never killed a German.

"*You* had better double up," said the Colonel. "It's time you killed one."

It came to Gilhooley's turn.

"How many men have you killed?" he was asked.

"In and out about fifty," was Gilhooley's answer.

"Make it a hundred then," said the Colonel; "and up you go, and the best of luck."

"By Jasus! I'll get fifty more out of it in no time," said Gilhooley, and on the following day he sauntered into the Cafe Pierre le Blanc in Nouex-les-Mines, drank another man's beer, and sat down on a chair at the table where four glasses filled to the brim stood sparkling in the lamplight.

Gilhooley, penniless and thirsty, had an unrivalled capacity for storing beer in his person.

"Back again, Gilhooley?" someone remarked in a diffident voice.'

"Back again!" said Gilhooley wearily, putting his hand in the pocket of his tunic and taking out a little round object about the size of a penny inkpot.

"I hear there's going to be a big push shortly," he muttered. "This," he said, holding the bomb between trigger finger and thumb, "will go bang into the enemy's trenches next charge."

A dozen horror-stricken eyes gazed at the bomb for a second, and the soldiers in the cafe remembered how Gilhooley once, in a moment of distraction, forgot that a fuse was lighted, then followed a hurried rush, and the cafe was almost deserted by the occupants. Gilhooley smiled wearily, replaced the bomb in his pocket, and set himself the task of draining the beer glasses.

My momentary thrill of terror died away when the bomb disappeared, and, leaving Bill, I approached the Wild Man's table and sat down.

"Gilhooley?" I said.

"Eh, what is it?" he interjected.

"Will you have a drink with me?" I hurried to inquire. "Something better than this beer for a change. Shall we try champagne?"

"Yes, we'll try it," he said sarcastically, and a queer smile hovered about his eyes. Somehow I had a guilty sense of doing a mean action.... I called to Bill.

"Come on, matey," I said.

Bill approached the table and sat down. I called for a bottle of champagne.

"This is Gilhooley, Bill," I said to my mate. "He's the bomber we've heard so much about."

"I suppose ye'll want to know everythin' about me now, seein' ye've asked me to take a drop of champagne," said Gilhooley, his voice rising. "Damn yer champagne. You think I'm a bloomin' alligator in the Zoo, d'ye? Give me a bun and I'll do anythin' ye want me to."

"That men should want to speak to you is merely due to your fame," I said. "In the dim recesses of the trenches men speak of your exploits with bated breath"

"What the devil are ye talkin' about?"

asked Gilhooley.

"About you," I said.

He burst out laughing at this and clinked glasses with me when we drank, but he seemed to forget Bill.

For the rest of the evening he was in high good humour, and before leaving he brought out his bomb and showed that it was only a dummy one, harmless as an egg-shell.

"But let me get half a dozen sergeants round a rum jar and out comes this bomb!" said Gilhooley. "Then they fly like hell and I get a double tot of rum."

"It's a damned good idea," I said. "What is he wanting?"

I pointed at the military policeman who had just poked his head through the cafe door. He looked round the room, taking stock of the occupants.

"All men of the London Irish must report to their companies at once," he shouted.

"There's somethin' on the blurry boards again," said Bill Teake. "I suppose we've got to get up to the trenches to-night. We were up last night diggin'," he said to 'Gilhooley.

Gilhooley shrugged his shoulders, took a stump of a cigarette from behind his ear and lit it.

"Take care of yourselves," he said as he went out.

At half-past nine we marched out of Nouexles-Mines bound for the trenches where we had to continue the digging which we had started the night before.

The brigade holding the firing line told us that the enemy were registering their range during the day, and the objective was the trench which we had dug on the previous night.... Then we knew that the work before us was fraught with danger; we would certainly be shelled when operations started. In single file, with rifles and picks over their shoulders, the boys went out into the perilous space between the lines. The night was grey with rain; not a star was visible in the drab expanse of cloudy sky, and the wet oozed from sandbag and dugout; the trench itself was sodden, and slush squirted about the boots that shuffled along; it was a miserable night. One of our men returned to the post occupied by the stretcher-bearers; he had become suddenly unwell with a violent pain in his stomach. We took him back to the nearest dressing-station and there he was put into an Engineers' wagon which was returning to the village in which our regiment was quartered.

Returning, I went out into the open between the lines. Our men were working across the front, little dark, blurred figures in the rainy greyness, picks and shovels were rising and falling, and lumps of earth were being flung out on to the grass. The enemy were already shelling on the left, the white flash of shrapnel and the red, lurid flames of bursting concussion shells lit up the night. So far the missiles were either falling short or overshooting their mark, and nobody had been touched. I just got to our company when the enemy began to shell it. There was a hurried flop to earth in the newly-dug holes, and I was immediately down flat on my face on top of several prostrate figures, a shrapnel burst in front, and a hail of singing bullets dug into the earth all round. A concussion shell raced past overhead and broke into splinters by the fire trench, several of the pieces whizzing back as far as the working party.

There followed a hail of shells, flash on flash, and explosion after explosion over our heads; the moment was a ticklish one, and I longed for the comparative safety of the fire trench. Why had I come out? I should have stopped with the other stretcher-bearers. But what did it matter? I was in no greater danger than any of my mates; what they had to stick I could stick, for the moment at least.

The shelling subsided as suddenly as it had begun. I got up again to find my attention directed towards something in front; a dark figure kneeling on the ground. I went forward and found a dead soldier, a Frenchman, a mere skeleton with the flesh eaten away from his face, leaning forward on his entrenching tool over a little hole that he had dug in the ground months before.

A tragedy was there, one of the sorrowful sights of war. The man, no doubt, had been in a charge—the French made a bayonet attack across this ground in the early part of last winter —and had been wounded. Immediately he was struck he got out his entrenching tool and endeavoured to dig himself in. A few shovelsful of earth were scooped out when a bullet struck him, and he leaned forward on his entrenching tool, dead. Thus I found him; and the picture in the grey night was one of a dead man resting for a moment as he dug his own grave.

"See that dead man?" I said to one of the digging party.

"H'm! there are hundreds of them lying here," was the answer, given almost indifferently. "I had to throw four to one side before I could start digging!"

I went back to the stretcher-bearers again; the men of my own company were standing under a shrapnel-proof bomb store, smoking and humming ragtime in low, monotonous voices. Musichall melodies are so melancholy at times, so full of pathos, especially on a wet night under shell fire.

"Where are the other stretcher-bearers?" I asked.

"They've gone out to the front to their companies," I was told. "Some of their men have been hit."

"Badly?"

"No one knows," was the answer. "Are our boys all right?"

"As far as I could see they're safe; but they're getting shelled in an unhealthy manner."

"They've left off firing now," said one of my mates. "You should've seen the splinters coming in here a minute ago, pit! pit! plop! on the sandbags. It's beastly out in the open."

A man came running along the trench, stumbled into our shelter, and sat down on a sandbag.

"You're the London Irish?" he asked. "Stretcher-bearers," I said. "Have you been out?"

"My God! I have," he answered. "'Tisn't half a do, either. A shell comes over and down I flops in the trench. My mate was standing on the parapet and down he fell atop of me. God! 'twasn't half a squeeze; I thought I was burst like a bubble.

'"Git off, matey,' I yells, 'I'm squeezed to death!'

"'Squeezed to death,' them was my words. But he didn't move, and something warm and sloppy ran down my face. It turned me sick.... I wriggled out from under and had a look.... He was dead, with half his head blown away.... Your boys are sticking to the work out there; just going on with the job as if nothing was amiss. When is the whole damned thing to come to a finish?"

A momentary lull followed, and a million sparks fluttered earthwards from a galaxy of searching star-shells.

"Why are such beautiful lights used in the killing of men?" I asked myself. Above in the quiet the gods were meditating, then, losing patience, they again burst into irrevocable rage, seeking, as it seemed, some obscure and fierce retribution.

The shells were loosened again; there was no escape from their frightful vitality, they crushed, burrowed, exterminated; obstacles were broken down, and men's lives were flicked out like flies off a window pane. A dug-out flew skywards, and the roof beams fell in the trench at our feet. We crouched under the bomb-shelter, mute, pale, hesitating. Oh! the terrible anxiety of men who wait passively for something to take place and always fearing the worst!"

"Stretcher-bearers at the double!"

We met him, crawling in on all fours like a beetle, the first case that came under our care. We dressed a stomach wound in the dug-out, and gave the boy two morphia tablets.... He sank into unconsciousness and never recovered. His grave is out behind the church of Loos-Gohelle, and his cap hangs on the arm of the cross that marks his sleeping place. A man had the calf of his right leg blown away; he died from shock; another got a bullet through his skull, another... But why enumerate how young lives were hurled away from young bodies?..

On the field of death, the shells, in colossal joy, chorused their terrible harmonies, making the heavens sonorous with their wanton and unbridled frenzy; star-shells, which seemed at times to be fixed on ceiling of the sky, oscillated in a dazzling whirl of red and green—and men died. ... We remained in the trenches the next day. They were very quiet, and we lay at ease in our dug-outs, read week-old papers, wrote letters and took turns on sentry-go. On our front lay a dull brown, monotonous level and two red-brick villages, Loos and Hulluch. Our barbed-wire entanglement, twisted and shell-scarred, showed countless rusty spikes which stuck out ominous and forbidding. A dead German hung on a wire prop, his feet caught in a *cheval de frise,* the skin of his face peeling away from his bones, and his hand clutching the wire as if for support. He had been out there for many months, a foolhardy foe who got a bullet through his head when examining our defences.

Here, in this salient, the war had its routine and habits, everything was done with regimental precision, and men followed the trade of arms as clerks follow their profession: to each man was allocated his post, he worked a certain number of hours, slept at stated times, had breakfast at dawn, lunch at noon, and tea at four. The ration parties called on the cave-dwellers with the promptitude of the butcher and baker, who attend to the needs of the villa-dwellers.

The postmen called at the dug-outs when dusk was settling, and delivered letters and parcels. Letter-boxes were placed in the parados walls and the hours of collection written upon them in pencil or chalk. Concerts were held in the big dug-outs, and little supper parties were fashionable when parcels were bulky. Tea was drunk in the open, the soldiers ate at looted tables, spread outside the dug-out doors. Over the "Savoy" a picture of the Mother of Perpetual Succour was to be seen and the boys who lived there swore that it brought them good luck; they always won at Banker and Brag. All shaved daily and washed with perfumed soaps.

The artillery exchanged shots every morning just to keep the guns clean. Sometimes a rifle shot might be heard, and we would ask, "Who is firing at the birds on the wire entanglements?" The days were peaceful then, but now all was different. The temper of the salient had changed.

In the distance we could see Lens, a mining town with many large chimneys, one of which was almost hidden in its own smoke. No doubt the Germans were working the coal mines. Loos looked quite small, there was a big slag-heap on its right, and on its left was a windmill with shattered wings. We had been shelling the village persistently for days, and, though it was not battered as Philosophe and Maroc were battered, many big, ugly rents and fractures were showing on the red-brick houses.

But it stood its beating well; it takes a lot of strafing to bring down even a jerry-built village. Houses built for a few hundred francs in times of peace, cost thousands of pounds to demolish in days of war. I suppose war is the most costly means of destruction.

Rumours flew about daily. Men spoke of a big push ahead, fixed the date for the great charge, and, as proof of their gossip, pointed at innumerable guns and wagons of shell which came through Les Brebis and Nouex-les-Mines daily. Even the Germans got wind of our activities, and in front of the blue-black slag-heap on the right of Loos they placed a large white board with the question written fair in big, black letters:

"WHEN IS THE BIG PUSH COMING OFF? WE ARE WAITING."

A well-directed shell blew the board to pieces ten minutes after it was put up.

I had a very nice dug-out in these trenches. It burrowed into the chalk, and its walls were as white as snow. When the candle was lit in the twilight, the most wonderfully soft shadows rustled over the roof and walls. The shadow of an elbow of chalk sticking out in the wall over my bed looked like the beak of a great formless vulture. On a closer examination I found that I had mistaken a wide-diffused bloodstain for a shadow. A man had come into the place once and he died there; his death was written in red on the wall.

I named the dug-out "The Last House

in the World." Was it not? It was the last tenanted house in our world.

Over the parapet of the trench was the Unknown with its mysteries deep as those of the grave.

CHAPTER III PREPARATIONS FOR LOOS

"Death will give us all a clean sheet."—Dudley Pryor. WE, the London Irish Rifles, know Les Brebis well, know every cafe and *estaminet,* every street and corner, every house, broken or sound, every washerwoman, wineshop matron, handy cook, and pretty girl. Time after time we have returned from the trenches to our old billet to find the good housewife up and waiting for us. She was a lank woman, made and clothed anyhow. Her garments looked as if they had been put on with a pitchfork. Her eyes protruded from their sockets, and one felt that if her tightly strained eyelids relaxed their grip for a moment the eyes would roll out on the floor. Her upper teeth protruded, and the point of her receding chin had lost itself somewhere in the hollow of her neck. Her pendant breasts hung flabbily, and it was a miracle how her youngest child, Gustave, a tot of seven months, could find any sustenance there. She had three children, who prattled all through the peaceful hours of the day. When the enemy shelled Les Brebis the children were bundled down into the cellar, and the mother went out to pick percussion caps from the streets. These she sold to officers going home on leave. The value of the percussion cap was fixed by the damage which the shell had done. A shell which fell on Les Brebis school and killed many men was picked up by this good woman, and at the present moment it is in my possession. We nicknamed this woman "Joan of Arc."

We had a delightful billet in this woman's house. We came in from war to find a big fire in the stove and basins of hot, steaming *cafe-aulait* on the table. If we returned from duty dripping wet through the rain, lines were hung across from wall to wall, and we knew that morning would find our muddy clothes warm and dry. The woman would count our number as we entered. One less than when we left! The missing man wore spectacles. She remembered him and all his mannerisms. He used to nurse her little baby boy, Gustave, and play games with the mite's toes. What had happened to him? He was killed by a shell, we told her. On the road to the trenches he was hit. Then a mist gathered in the woman's eyes, and two tears rolled down her cheeks. We drank our *cafe-au-laiP.* "Combien, madam?"

"Souvenir," was the reply through sobs, and we thanked her for the kindness. Upstairs we bundled into our room, and threw our equipment down on the clean wooden floor, lit a candle and undressed. All wet clothes were flung downstairs, where the woman would hang them up to dry. Everything was the same here as when we left; save where the last regiment had, in a moment of inspiration, chronicled its deeds in verse on the wall. Pryor, the lance-corporal, read the poem aloud to us:

"Gentlemen, the Guards,
When the brick fields they took
The Germans took the hook
And left the Gentlemen in charge."

The soldiers who came and went voiced their griefs on this wall, but in latrine language and Rabelaisian humour. Here were three proverbs written in a shaky hand:

"The Army pays good money, but little of it."

"In the Army you are sertin to receive what you get."

"The wages of sin and a soldir is death."

Under these was a couplet written by a fatalist:

"I don't care if the Germans come,
If I have an extra tot of rum."

Names of men were scrawled everywhere on the wall, from roof to floor. Why have some men this desire to scrawl their names on every white surface they see, I often wonder? One of my mates, who wondered as I did, finally found expression in verse, which glared forth accusingly from the midst of the riot of names in the room:

"A man's ambition must be small
Who writes his name upon this wall,
And well he does deserve his pay
A measly, mucky bob a day."

The woman never seemed to mind this scribbling on the wall; in Les Brebis they have to put up with worse than this. The house of which I speak is the nearest inhabited one to the firing line. Half the houses in the street are blown down, and every ruin has its tragedy. The natives are gradually getting thinned out by the weapons of war. The people refuse to quit their homes. This woman has a sister in Nouex-lesMines, a town five kilometres further away from the firing line, but she refused to go there. "The people of Nouex-les-Mines are no good," she told us. "I would not be where they are. Nobody can trust them."

The history of Les Brebis must, if written, be written in blood. The washerwoman who washed our shirts could tell stories of adventure that would eclipse tales of romance as the sun eclipses a brazier. Honesty and fortitude are the predominant traits of the Frenchwoman.

Once I gave the washerwoman my cardigan jacket to wash, and immediately afterwards we were ordered off to the trenches. When we left the firing line we went back to Nouex-les-Mines. A month passed before the regiment got to Les Brebis again. The washerwoman called at my billet and brought back the cardigan jacket, also a franc piece which she had found in the pocket. On the day following the woman was washing her baby at a pump in the street and a shell blew her head off. Pieces of the child were picked up a hundred yards away. The washerwoman's second husband (she had been married twice) was away at the war; all that remained in the household now was a daughter whom Pryor, with his nicknaming craze, dubbed "Mercedes."

But here in Les Brebis, amidst death and desolation, wont and use held their sway. The cataclysm of a continent had not changed the ways and manners of the villagers, they took things phlegmatically, with fatalistic calm. The children played in the gutters of the streets, lovers met beneath the stars and told the story of ancient passion, the miser hoarded his money, the preacher spoke to his Sunday congregation, and the plate was handed round for the worshippers' sous, men and women died natural deaths, children were born, females chattered at the street pumps and circulated rumours about their neighbours... . All this when wagons of shells passed through the streets all day and big guns travelled up nearer the lines every night. Never had Les Brebis known such traffic. Horses, limbers and ''guns, guns, limbers and horses going and coming from dawn to dusk and from dusk to dawn. From their emplacements in every spinney and every hollow in the fields the guns spoke earnestly and continuously. Never had guns voiced such a threat before. They were everywhere; could there be room for another in all the spaces of Les Brebis and our front line? It was impossible to believe it, but still they came up, monsters with a mysterious air of detachment perched on limbers with caterpillar wheels, little field guns that flashed metallic glints to the cafe lamps, squat trench howitzers on steel platforms impassive as toads....

The coming and passing was a grand poem, and the poem found expression in clanging and rattle in the streets of Les Brebis through the days and nights of August and September, 1915. For us, we worked in our little ways, dug advanced trenches under shell fire in a field where four thousand dead Frenchmen were wasting to clay. These men had charged last winter and fell to maxim and rifle fire; over their bodies we were to charge presently and take Loos and the trenches behind. The London Irish were to cross the top in the first line of attack, so the rumour said.

One evening, when dusk was settling in the streets, when ruined houses assumed fantastic shapes, and spirits seemed to be lurking in the shattered piles, we went up the streets of Les Brebis on our way to the trenches. Over by the church of Les Brebis, the spire of which was sharply defined in the clear air, the shells were bursting and the smoke of the explosions curled above the red roofs of the houses. The enemy was bombarding the road ahead, and the wounded were being carried back to the dressing stations. We met many stretchers on the road. The church of Bully-Grenay had been hit, and a barn near the church had been blown in on top of a platoon of soldiers which occupied it. We had to pass the church. The whole battalion seemed to be very nervous, and a presentiment of something evil seemed to fill the minds of the men. The mood was not of common occurrence, but this unaccountable depression permeates whole bodies of men at times.

We marched in silence, hardly daring to breathe. Ahead, under a hurricane of shell, Bully-Grenay was withering to earth. The night itself was dark and subdued, not a breeze stirred in the poplars which lined the long, straight road. Now and again, when a star-shell flamed over the firing line, we caught a glimpse of Bully-Grenay, huddled and helpless, its houses battered, its church riven, its chimneys fractured and lacerated. We dreaded passing the church; the cobbles on the roadway there were red with the blood of men.

We got into the village, which was deserted even by the soldiery; the civil population had left the place weeks ago. We reached the church, and there, arm in arm, we encountered a French soldier and a young girl. They took very little notice of us, they were deep in sweet confidences which only the young can exchange. The maiden was "Mercedes. " The sight was good; it was as a tonic to us. A load seemed to have been lifted off our shoulders, and we experienced a light and airy sensation of heart. We reached the trenches without mishap, and set about our work. The enemy spotted us digging a new sap, and he began to shell with more than usual vigour. We were rather unlucky, for four of our men were killed and nine or ten got wounded.

Night after night we went up to the trenches and performed our various duties. Keeps and redoubts were strengthened and four machine guns were placed where only one stood before. Always while we worked the artillery on both sides conducted a loud-voiced argument; concussion shells played havoc with masonry, and shrapnel shells flung their deadly freight on roads where the transports hurried, and where the longeared mules sweated in the traces of the limbers of war. We spoke of the big work ahead, but up till the evening preceding Saturday, September 25th, we were not aware of the part which we had to play in the forthcoming event. An hour before dusk our officer read instructions, and outlined the plan of the main attack, which would start at dawn on the following day, September 25th, 1915.

In co-operation with an offensive movement by the 10th French Army on our right, the 1st and 4th Army Corps were to attack the enemy from a point opposite Bully-Grenay on the south to the La Bassee Canal on the north. We had dug the assembly trenches on our right opposite Bully-Grenay; that was to be the starting point for the 4th Corps— our Corps. Our Division, the 47th London, would lead the attack of the 4th Army Corps, and the London Irish would be the first in the fight. Our objective was the second German trench which lay just in front of Loos village and a mile away from our own first line trench. Every movement of the operations had been carefully planned, and nothing was left to chance. Never had we as many guns as now, and these guns had been bombarding the enemy's positions almost incessantly for ten days. Smoke bombs would be used. The thick fumes resulting from their explosion between the lines would cover our advance. At five o'clock all our guns, great and small, would open up a heavy fire. Our aircraft had located most of the enemy's batteries, and our heavy guns would be trained on these until they put them out of action. Five minutes past six our guns would lengthen their range and shell the enemy's reserves, and at the same moment our regiment would get clear of the trenches and advance in four lines in extended order with a second's interval between the lines. The advance must be made in silence at a steady pace.

Stretcher bearers had to cross with their companies; none of the attacking party must deal with the men who fell out on the way across. A party would be detailed out to attend to the wounded who fell near the assembly trenches.... The attack had been planned with such intelligent foresight that our casualties would be very few. The job before us was quite easy and simple.

"What do you think of it?" I asked my mate, Bill Teake. "I think a bottle of champagne would be very nice."

"Just what I thought myself," said Bill. "I see Dudley Pryor is off to the cafe already. I've no money. I'm pore as a mummy."

"You got paid yesterday," I said with a laugh. "You get poor very quickly."

An embarrassed smile fluttered around his lips.

"A man gets pore 'cordin' to no rule," he replied. "Leastways, I do."

"Well, I've got a lot of francs," I said. "We may as well spend it."

"You're damned right," he answered. "Maybe we'll not 'ave a chance to"

"It doesn't matter a damn whether"

"The officer says it will be an easy job. I don't know the"

He paused. We understood things half spoken.

"Champagne?" I hinted.

"Nothing like champagne," said Bill.

CHAPTER IV BEFORE THE CHARGE
Before I joined the Army I lived in Donegal,
Where every night the Fairies,
 Would hold their carnival.
But now I'm out in Flanders,
Where men like wheat-ears fall,
 And it's Death and not the Fairies
 Who is holding carnival.

IPOKED my head through the upper window of our billet and looked down the street. An ominous calm brooded over the village, the trees which lined the streets stood immovable in the darkness, with lone shadows clinging to the trunks. On my right, across a little rise, was the firing line. In the near distance was the village of Bully-Grenay, roofless and tenantless, and further off was Philosophe, the hamlet with its dark-blue slag-heap bulking large against the horizon. Souchez in the hills was as usual active; a heavy artillery engagement was in progress.

White and lurid splashes of flame dabbed at the sky, and the smoke, rising from the ground, paled in the higher air; but the breeze blowing away from me carried the tumult and thunder far from my ears. I looked on a conflict without sound; a furious fight seen but unheard.

A coal-heap near the village stood, colossal and threatening; an engine shunted a long row of wagons along the railway line which fringed Les Brebis. In a pit by the mine a big gun began to speak loudly, and the echo of its voice palpitated through the room and dislodged a tile from the roof.... My mind was suddenly permeated by a feeling of proximity to the enemy. He whom we were going to attack at dawn seemed to be very close to me. I could almost feel his presence in the room. At dawn I might deprive him of life and he might deprive me of mine. Two beings give life to a man, but one can deprive him of it. Which is the greater mystery? Birth or death? They who are responsible for the first may take pleasure, but who can glory in the second?... To kill a man.... To feel for ever after the deed that you have deprived a fellow being of life!

"We're beginning to strafe again," said Pryor, coming to my side as a second reverberation shook the house. "It doesn't matter. I've got a bottle of champagne and a box of cigars."

"I've got a bottle as well," I said.

"There'll be a hell of a do to-morrow," said Pryor.

"I suppose there will," I replied. "The officer said that our job will be quite an easy one." "H'm!" said Pryor.

I looked down at the street and saw Bill Teake. "There's Bill down there," I remarked. "He's singing a song. Listen."

"'I like your smile,
I like your style,
I like your soft blue dreamy eyes'"

"There's passion in that voice," I said. "Has he fallen in love again?"

A cork went plunk! from a bottle behind me, and Pryor from the shadows of the room answered, "Oh, yes! He's in love again; the girl next door is his fancy now."

"Oh, so it seems," I said. "She's out at the pump now and Bill is edging up to her as quietly as if he were going to loot a chicken off its perch."

Bill is a boy for the girls; he finds a new love at every billet. His fresh flame was a squat stump of a Millet girl in short petticoats and stout sabots. Her eyes were a deep black, her teeth very white. She was a comfortable, goodnatured girl, "a big 'andful of love," as he said himself, but she was not very good-looking.

Bill sidled up to her side and fixed an earnest gaze on the water falling from the pump; then he nudged the girl in the hip with a playful hand and ran his fingers over the back of her neck.

"Allez vous en!" she cried, but otherwise made no attempt to resist Bill's advances.

"Allez voos ong yerself!" said Bill, and burst into song again.

"'She's the pretty little girl from Nowhere,
Nowhere at all.
She's the'"

He was unable to resist the temptation any longer, and he clasped the girl round the waist and planted a kiss on her cheek. The maiden did not relish this familiarity. Stooping down she placed her hand in the pail, raised a handful of water and flung it in Bill's face. The Cockney retired crestfallen and spluttering, and a few minutes afterwards he entered the room.

"Yes, I think that there are no women on earth to equal them," said Pryor to me, deep in a prearranged conversation. "They have a grace of their own and a coyness which I admire. I don't think that any women are like the women of France."

"'Oo?" asked Bill Teake, sitting down on the floor.

"Pat and I are talking about the French girls," said Pryor. "They're splendid."

"H'm!" grunted Bill in a colourless voice.

"Not much humbug about them," I remarked.

"I prefer English gals," said Bill. "They can make a joke and take one. As for the French gals, ugh!"

"But they're not all alike," I said. "Some may resent advances in the street, and show a temper when they're kissed over a pump."

"The water from the Les Brebis pumps is very cold," said Pryor.

We could not see Bill's face in the darkness, but we could almost feel our companion squirm.

"'Ave yer got some champagne, Pryor?" he asked with studied indifference. "My froat's like sandpaper."

"Plenty of champagne, matey," said Pryor in a repentant voice. "We're all going to get drunk to-night. Are you?"

"Course I am," said Bill. "It's very comfy to 'ave a drop of champagne."

"More comfy than a kiss even," said Pryor.

As he spoke the door was shoved inwards and our corporal entered. For a moment he stood there without speaking, his long, lank form darkly outlined against the half light.

"Well, corporal?" said Pryor interrogatively.

"Why don't you light a candle?" asked the corporal. "I thought that we were going to get one another's addresses."

"So we were," I said, as if just remembering a decision arrived at a few hours previously. But I had it in my mind all the time.

Bill lit a candle and placed it on the floor while I covered up the window with a ground sheet. The window looked out on the firing line three kilometres away, and the light, if uncovered, might be seen by the enemy. I glanced down the street and saw boys in khaki strolling aimlessly about, their cigarettes glowing.... The starshells rose in the sky out behind Bully-Grenay, and again I had that feeling of the enemy's presence which was mine a few moments before.

Kore, another of our section, returned from a neighbouring cafe, a thoughtful look in his dark eyes and a certain irresolution in his movements. His delicate nostrils and pale lips quivered nervously, betraying doubt and a little fear of the work ahead at dawn. Under his arm he carried a bottle of champagne which he placed on the floor beside the candle. Sighing a little, he lay down at full length on the floor, not before he brushed the dust aside with a newspaper. Kore was very neat and took great pride in his uniform, which fitted him like an eyelid.

Felan and M'Crone came in together, arm in arm. The latter was in a state of subdued excitement; his whole body shook as if he were in fever; when he spoke his voice was highly pitched and unnatural, a sign that he was under the strain of great nervous tension. Felan looked very much at ease, though now and again he fumbled with the pockets of his tunic, buttoning and unbuttoning the flaps and digging his hands into his pockets as if for something which was not there. He had no cause for alarm; he was the company cook and, according to regulations, would not cross in the charge.

"Blimey! you're not 'arf a lucky dawg!" said Bill, glancing at Felan. "I wish I was the cook to-morrow."

"I almost wish I was myself."

"Wot d'yer mean?"

"Do you expect an Irishman is going to cook bully-beef when his regiment goes over the top?" asked Felan. "For shame!"

We rose, all of us, shook him solemnly by the hand, and wished him luck.

"Now, what about the addresses?" asked Kore. "It's time we wrote them down."

"It's as well to get it over," I said, but no one stirred. We viewed the job with distrust. By doing it we reconciled ourselves to a dread inevitable; the writing of these addresses seemed to be the only thing that stood between us and death. If we could only put it off for another little while....

"We'll 'ave a drink to 'elp us," said Bill, and a cork went plonk! The bottle was handed round, and each of us, except the corporal, drank in turn until the bottle was emptied. The corporal was a teetotaller.

"Now we'll begin," I said. The wine had given me strength. "If I'm killed write to and , tell them that my death was sudden—easy."

"That's the thing to tell them," said the corporal. "It's always best to tell them at home that death was sudden and painless. It's not much of a consolation, but"

He paused.

"It's the only thing one can do," said Felan.

"I've nobody to write to," said Pryor, when his turn came. "There's a Miss. But what the devil does it matter! I've nobody to write to, nobody that cares a damn what becomes of me," he concluded. "At least I'm not like Bill," he added.

"And who will I write to for you, Bill?" I asked.

Bill scratched his little white potato of a nose, puckered his lips, and became thoughtful. I suddenly realised that Bill was very dear to me.

"Not afraid, matey?" I asked.

"Naw," he answered in a thoughtful voice.

"A man has only to die once, anyhow," said Felan.

"Greedy! 'Ow many times d'yer want ter die?" asked Bill. "But I s'pose if a man 'ad nine lives like a cat 'e wouldn't mind dyin' once."

"But suppose," said Pryor.

"S'pose," muttered Bill. "Well, if it 'as got to be it can't be 'elped.... I'm not goin' to give any address to anybody," he said. "I'm goin' to 'ave a drink."

We were all seated on the floor round the candle which was stuck in the neck of an empty champagne bottle. The candle flickered faintly, and the light made feeble fight with the shadows in the corners. The room was full of the aromatic flavour of Turkish cigarettes and choice cigars, for money was spent that evening with the recklessness of men going out to die. Teake handed round a fresh bottle of champagne and I gulped down a mighty mouthful. My shadow, flung by the candle on the white wall, was a grotesque caricature, my nose stretched out like a beak, and a monstrous bottle was tilted on demoniac lips. Pryor pointed at it with his trigger finger, laughed, and rose to give a quotation from Omar, forgot the quotation, and sat down again. Kore was giving his home address to the corporal, Bill's hand trembled as he raised a match to his cigar. Pryor was on his feet again, handsome Pryor, with a college education.

"What does death matter?" he said. "It's as natural to die as it is to be born, and perhaps the former is the easier event of the two. We have no remembrance of birth and will carry no remembrance of death across the bourne from which there is no return. Do you know what Epictetus said about death, Bill?"

"Wot regiment was 'e in?" asked Bill.

"He has been dead for some eighteen hundred years."

"Oh! blimey!"

"Epictetus said, 'Where death is I am not, where death is not I am,'" Pryor continued. "Death will give us all a clean sheet. If the sergeant who issues short rum rations dies on the field of honour (don't drink all the champagne, Bill) we'll talk of him when he's gone as a damned good fellow, but alive we've got to borrow epithets from Bill's vocabulary of vituperation to speak of the aforesaid non-commissioned abomination."

"Is 'e callin' me names, Pat?" Bill asked me.

I did not answer for the moment, for Bill was undergoing a strange transformation. His head was increasing in size, swelling up until it almost filled the entire room. His little potato of a nose assumed fantastic dimensions. The other occupants of the room diminished in bulk and receded into far distances. I tried to attract Pryor's attention to the phenomenon, but the youth receding with the others was now balancing a champagne bottle on his nose, entirely oblivious of his surroundings.

"Be quiet, Bill," I said, speaking with difficulty. "Hold your tongue!"

I began to feel drowsy, but another mouthful of champagne renewed vitality in my body. With this feeling came a certain indifference towards the morrow. I must confess that up to now I had a vague distrust of my actions in the work ahead. My normal self revolted at the thought of the coming dawn; the experiences of my life had not prepared me for one day of savage and ruthless butchery. To-morrow I had to go forth prepared to do much that I disliked.... I had another sip of wine; we were at the last bottle now.

Pryor looked out of the window, raising the blind so that little light shone out into the darkness.

"A Scottish division are passing through the street, in silence, their kilts swinging," he said. "My God! it does look fine." He arranged the blind again and sat down. Bill was cutting a sultana cake in neat portions and handing them round.

"Come, Felan, and sing a song," said M'Crone.

"My voice is no good now," said Felan, but by his way of speaking, we knew that he would oblige.

"Now, Felan, come along!" we chorused.

Felan wiped his lips with the back of his hand, took a cigar between his fingers and thumb and put it out by rubbing the lighted end against his trousers. Then he placed the cigar behind his ear.

"Well, what will I sing?" he asked.

"Any damned thing," said Bill.

"'The Trumpeter,' and we'll all help," said Kore.

Felan leant against the wall, thrust his head back, closed his eyes, stuck the thumb of his right hand into a buttonhole of his tunic and began his song.

His voice, rather hoarse, but very pleasant, faltered a little at first, but was gradually permeated by a note of deepest feeling, and a strange, unwonted passion surged through the melody. Felan was pouring his soul into the song. A moment ago the singer was one with us; now he gave himself up to the song, and the whole lonely romance of war, its pity and its pain, swept through the building and held us in its spell. Kore's mobile nostrils quivered. M'Crone shook as if with ague. We all listened, enraptured, our eyes shut as the singer's were, to the voice that quivered through the smoky room. I could not help feeling that Felan himself listened to his own song, as something which was no part of him, but which affected him strangely.

"'Trumpeter, what are you sounding now?

Is it the call I'm seeking?'

'Lucky for you if you hear it all

For my trumpet's but faintly speaking—

I'm calling 'em home. Come home! Come home!

Tread light o'er the dead in the valley,

Who are lying around

Face down to the ground,

And they can't hear '"

Felan broke down suddenly, and, coming across the floor, he entered the circle and sat down.

"'Twas too high for me," he muttered huskily. "My voice has gone to the dogs.... One time"

Then he relapsed into silence. None of us spoke, but we were aware that Felan knew how much his song had moved us.

"Have another drink," said Pryor suddenly, in a thick voice. "'Look not upon the wine when it is red,' " he quoted. "But there'll be something redder than wine to-morrow!"

"I wish we fought wiv bladders on sticks; it would be more to my taste," said Bill Teake.

"Ye're not having a drop at all, corporal," said M'Crone. "Have a sup; it's grand stuff."

The corporal shook his head. He sat on the floor with his back against the wall, his hands under his thighs. He had a blunt nose with wide nostrils, and his grey, contemplative eyes kept roving slowly round the circle as if he were puzzling over our fate in the charge to-morrow.

"I don't drink," he said. "If I can't do without it now after keeping off it so long, I'm not much good."

"Yer don't know wot's good for yer," said Bill, gazing regretfully at the last half-bottle. "There's nuffink like fizz. My ole man's a devil fer 'is suds; so'm I."

The conversation became riotous, questions and replies got mixed and jumbled. "I suppose we'll get to the front trench anyhow; maybe to the second. But we'll get flung back from that.

" "Wish we'd another bloomin' bottle of fizz." "S'pose our guns will not lift their range quick enough when we advance. We'll have any amount of casualties with our own shells." "The sergeant says that our objective is the crucifix in Loos churchyard." "Imagine killing men right up to the foot of the Cross."...

Our red-headed platoon sergeant appeared at the top of the stairs, his hair lurid in the candle light.

"Enjoying yourselves, boys?" he asked, with paternal solicitude. The sergeant's heart was in his platoon. "'Avin' a bit of a frisky," said Bill. "Will yer 'ave a drop?"

"I don't mind," said the sergeant. He spoke almost in a whisper, and something seemed to be gripping at his throat.

He put the bottle to his lips and paused for a moment.

"Good luck to us all!" he said, and drank.

"We're due to leave in fifteen minutes," he told us. "Be ready when you hear the whistle blown in the street. Have a smoke now, for no pipes or cigarettes are to be lit on the march."

He paused for a moment, then, wiping his moustache with the back of his hand, he clattered downstairs.

The night was calm and full of enchantment. The sky hung low and was covered with a greyish haze. We marched past Les Brebis Church up a long street where most of the houses were levelled to the ground. Ahead the star-shells rioted in a blaze of colour, and a few rifles were snapping viciously out by Hohenzollern Redoubt, and a building on fire flared lurid against the eastern sky. Apart from that silence and suspense, the world waited breathlessly for some great event. The big guns lurked on their emplacements, and now and again we passed a dark-blue muzzle peeping out from its cover, sentinel, as it seemed, over the neatly piled stack of shells which would furnish it with its feed at dawn.

At the fringe of Bully-Grenay we left the road and followed a straggling path across the level fields where telephone wires had fallen down and lay in wait to trip unwary feet. Always the whispers were coming down the line: "Mind the wires!" "Mind the shell-holes!" "Gunpit on the left. Keep clear." "Mind the dead mule on the right," etc.

Again we got to the road where it runs into the village of Maroc. A church stood at the entrance and it was in a wonderful state of preservation. Just as we halted for a moment on the roadway the enemy sent a solitary shell across which struck the steeple squarely, turning it round, but failing to overthrow it.

"A damned good shot," said Pryor approvingly.

CHAPTER V OVER THE TOP
Was it only yesterday
Lusty comrades marched away?
Now they're covered up with clay.
Hearty comrades these have been,
But no more will they be seen
Drinking wine at Nouex-les-Mines.

BRAZIER glowed on the floor of the trench and I saw fantastic figures in the red blaze; the interior ot a vast church lit up with a myriad candles, and dark figures kneeling in prayer in front of their plaster saints. The edifice was an enchanted Fairyland, a poem of striking contrasts in light and shade. I peered over the top. The air blazed with star-shells, and Loos in front stood out like a splendid dawn. A row of impassive faces, sleep-heavy they looked, lined our parapet; bayonets, silver-spired, stood up over the sandbags; the dark bays, the recessed dug-outs with their khaki-clad occupants dimly defined in the light of little candles took on fantastic shapes. From the North Sea to the Alps stretched a line of men who could, if they so desired, clasp one another's hands all the way along. A joke which makes men laugh at Ypres at dawn may be told on sentry-go at Souchez by dusk, and the laugh which accompanies it ripples through the long, deep trenches of Cuinchy, the breastworks of Richebourg and the chalk alleys of Vermelles until it breaks itself like a summer wave against the traverse where England ends and France begins.

Many of our men were asleep, and maybe dreaming. What were their dreams?... I could hear faint, indescribable rustlings as the winds loitered across the levels in front; a light shrapnel shell burst, and its smoke quivered in the radiant light of the star-shells. Showers and sparks fell from high up and died away as they fell. Like lives of men, I thought, and again that feeling of proximity to the enemy surged through me.

A boy came along the trench carrying a football under his arm. "What are you going to do with that?" I asked.

"It's some idea, this," he said with a laugh.' "We're going to kick it across into the German trench."

"It *is* some idea," I said. "What are our chances of victory in the game?"

"The playing will tell," he answered enigmatically. "It's about four o'clock now," he added, paused and became thoughtful. The mention of the hour suggested something to him....

I could now hear the scattered crackling of guns as they called to one another saying: "It's time to be up and doing!" The brazen monsters of many a secret emplacement were registering their range, rivalry in their voices. For a little the cock-crowing of artillery went on, then suddenly a thousand roosts became alive and voluble, each losing its own particular sound as all united in one grand concert of fury. The orchestra of war swelled in an incessant fanfare of dizzy harmony. Floating, stuttering, whistling, screaming and thundering the clamorous voices belched into a rich gamut of passion which shook the grey heavens. The sharp, zigzagging sounds of high velocity shells cut through the pandemonium like forked lightning, and far away, as it seemed, sounding like a distant breakwater the big missiles from caterpillar howitzers lumbered through the higher deeps of the sky. The brazen lips of death cajoled, threatened, whispered, whistled, laughed and sung: here were the sinister and sullen voices of destruction, the sublime and stupendous paean of power intermixed in sonorous clamour and magnificent vibration.

Felan came out into the trench. He had been asleep in his dug-out. "I can't make tea now," he said, fumbling with his mess-tin. "We'll soon have to get over the top. Murdagh, Nobby Byrne and Corporal Clancy are here," he remarked.

"They are in hospital," I said.

"They were," said Felan; "but the hospitals have been cleared out to make room for men wounded in the charge. The three boys were ordered to go further back to be out of the way, but they asked to be allowed to join in the charge, and they are here now."

He paused for a moment. "Good luck to you, Pat," he said with a strange catch in his voice. "I hope you get through all right."

A heavy rifle fire was opened by the Germans and the bullets snapped viciously at our sandbags. Such little things bullets seemed in the midst of all the pandemonium! But bigger stuff was coming. Twenty yards away a shell dropped on a dug-out and sandbags and occupants whirled up in mid-air. The call for stretcher-bearers came to my bay, and I rushed round the traverse towards the spot where help was required accompanied by two others. A shrapnel shell burst overhead and the man in front of me fell. I bent to lift him, but he stumbled to his feet. The concussion had knocked him down; he was little the worse for his accident, but he felt a bit shaken. The other stretcher-bearer was bleeding at the cheek and temple, and I took him back to a sound dug-out and dressed his wound. He was in great pain, but very brave, and when another stricken boy came in he set about dressing him. I went outside into the trench. A perfect hurricane of shells was coming across, concussion shells that whirled the sandbags broadcast and shrapnel that burst high in air and shot their freight to earth with resistless precipitancy; bombs whirled in air and burst when they found earth with an ear-splitting clatter. "Out in the open!" I muttered and tried not to think too clearly of what would happen when we got out there.

It was now grey day, hazy and moist, and the thick clouds of pale yellow smoke curled high in space and curtained the dawn off from the scene of war. The word was passed along. "London Irish lead on to assembly trench." The assembly trench was in front, and there the scaling ladders were placed against the parapet, ready steps to death, as someone remarked. I had a view of the men swarming up the ladders when I got there, their bayonets held in steady hands, and at a little distance off a football swinging by its whang from a bayonet standard.

The company were soon out in the open marching forward. The enemy's guns were busy, and the rifle and maxim bullets ripped the sandbags. The infantry fire was wild but of slight intensity. The enemy could not see the attacking party. But, judging by the row, it was hard to think that men could weather the leaden storm in the open.

The big guns were not so vehement now, our artillery had no doubt played havoc with the hostile batteries.... I went to the foot of a ladder and got hold of a rung. A soldier in front was clambering across. Suddenly he dropped backwards and bore me to the ground; the bullet caught him in the forehead. I got to my feet to find a stranger in grey uniform coming down the ladder. He reached the floor of the trench, put up his hands when I looked at him and cried in a weak, imploring voice, "Kamerad! Kamerad!"

"A German!" I said to my mate.

"H'm! h'm!" he answered.

I flung my stretcher over the parapet, and, followed by my comrade stretcher-bearer, I clambered up the ladder and went over the top.

CHAPTER VI ACROSS THE OPEN

"The firefly lamps were lighted yet,
As we crossed the top of the parapet,
But the East grew pale to another fire,
As our bayonets gleamed by the foeman's wire.
And the Eastern sky was gold and grey.
And under our feet the dead men lay,
As we entered Loos in the morning."

HE moment had come when it was unwise to think. The country round Loos was like a sponge; the god of war had stamped with his foot on it, and thousands of men, armed, ready to kill, were squirted out on to the level, barren fields of danger. To dwell for a moment on the novel position of being standing where a thousand deaths swept by, missing you by a mere hair's breadth, would be sheer folly. There on the open field of death my life was out of my keeping, but the sensation of fear never entered my being. There was so much simplicity and so little effort in doing what I had done, in doing what eight hundred comrades had done, that I felt I could carry through the work before me with as much credit as my code of self respect required. The maxims went crackle like dry brushwood under the feet of a marching host. A bullet passed very close to my face like a sharp, sudden breath; a second hit the ground in front, flicked up a little shower of dust, and ricochetted to the left, hitting the earth many times before it found a resting place. The air was vicious with bullets; a million invisible birds flicked their wings very close to my face. Ahead the clouds of smoke, sluggish low-lying fog, and fumes of bursting shells, thick in volume, receded towards the German trenches, and formed a striking background for the soldiers who were marching up a low slope towards the enemy's parapet, which the smoke still hid from view. There was no haste in the forward move, every step was taken with regimental precision, and twice on the way across the Irish boys halted for a moment to correct their alignment. Only at a point on the right there was some confusion and a little irregularity. Were the men wavering? No fear! The boys on the right were dribbling the elusive football towards the German trench.

Raising the stretcher, my mate and I went forward. For the next few minutes I was conscious of many things. A slight rain was falling; the smoke and fumes I saw had drifted back, exposing a dark streak on the field of green, the enemy's trench. A little distance away from me three men hurried forward, and two of them carried a box of rifle ammunition. One of the bearers fell flat to earth, his two mates halted for a moment, looked at the stricken boy, and seemed to puzzle at something. Then they caught hold of the box hangers and rushed forward. The man on the ground raised himself on his elbow and looked after his mates; then sank down again to the wet ground. Another soldier came crawling towards us on his belly, looking for all the world like a gigantic lobster which had escaped from its basket. His lower lip, was cut clean to the chin and hanging apart; blood welled through the muddy khaki trousers where they covered the hips.

I recognised the fellow.

"Much hurt, matey?" I asked.

"I'll manage to get in," he said.

"Shall I put a dressing on?" I inquired.

"IH manage to get into our own trench," he stammered, spitting the blood from his lips.

"There are others out at the wires. S has caught it bad. Try and get him in, Pat."

"Right, old man," I said, as he crawled off. "Good luck."

My cap was blown off my head as if by a violent gust of wind, and it dropped on the ground. I put it on again, and at that moment a shell burst near at hand and a dozen splinters sung by my ear. I walked forward with a steady step.

"What took my cap off?" I asked myself. "It went away just as if it was caught in a breeze. God!" I muttered, in a burst of realisation, "it was that shell passing." I breathed very deeply, my blood rushed down to my toes and an airy sensation filled my body. Then the stretcher dragged.

"Lift the damned thing up," I called to my mate over my shoulder. There was no reply. I looked round to find him gone, either mixed up in a whooping rush of kilted Highlanders, who had lost their objective and were now charging parallel to their own trench, or perhaps he got killed.... How strange that the Highlanders could not charge in silence, I thought, and then recollected that most of my boyhood friends, Donegal lads, were in Scottish regiments.... I placed my stretcher on my shoulder, walked forward towards a bank of smoke which seemed to be standing stationary, and came across our platoon sergeant and part of his company.

"Are we going wrong, or are the Jocks wrong?" he asked his men, then shouted, "Lie flat, boys, for a minute, until we see where we are. There's a big crucifix in Loos churchyard, and we've got to draw on that."

The men threw themselves flat; the sergeant went down on one knee and leant forward on his rifle, his hands on the bayonet' standard, the fingers pointing upwards and the palms pressed close to the sword which was covered with rust.... How hard it would be to draw it from a dead body!... The sergeant seemed to be kneeling in prayer.... In front the cloud cleared away, and the black crucifix standing over the graves of Loos became revealed.

"Advance, boys!" said the sergeant. "Steady on to the foot of the Cross and rip the swine out of their trenches."

The Irish went forward....

A boy sat on the ground bleeding at the shoulder and knee.

"You've got hit," I said.

"In a few places," he answered, in a very matter-of-fact voice. "I want to get into a shellhole."

"I'll try and get you into one," I said. "But I want someone to help me. Hi! you there! Come and give me a hand."

I spoke to a man who sat on the rim of a crater near at hand. His eyes, set close in a white, ghastly face, stared tensely at me. He sat in-a crouching position, his head thrust forward, his right hand gripping tightly at a mud-stained rifle. Presumably he was a bit shaken and was afraid to advance further.

"Help me to get this fellow into a shell-hole," I called. "He can't move."

There was no answer.

"Come along," I cried, and then it was suddenly borne to me that the man was dead. I dragged the wounded boy into the crater and dressed his wounds.

A shell struck the ground in front, burrowed, and failed to explode.

"Thank Heaven!" I muttered, and hurried ahead. Men and pieces of men were lying all over the place. A leg, an arm, then again a leg, cut off at the hip. A finely formed leg, the latter, gracefully putteed. A dummy leg in a tailor's window could not be more graceful. It might be X; he was an artist in dress, a Beau Brummel in khaki. Fifty yards further along I found the rest of X....

The harrowing sight was repellent, antagonistic to my mind. The tortured things lying at my feet were symbols of insecurity, ominous reminders of danger from which no discretion could save a man. My soul was barren of pity; fear went down into the innermost parts of me, fear for myself. The dead and dying lay all around me; I felt a vague obligation to the latter; they must be carried out. But why should I trouble! Where could I begin? Everything was so far apart. I was too puny to start my labours in such a derelict world. The difficulty of accommodating myself to an old task under new conditions was enormous.

A figure in grey, a massive block of Bavarian bone and muscle, came running towards me, his arms in air, and Bill Teake following him with a long bayonet.

"A prisoner!" yelled the boy on seeing me. "'Kamerad! Kamerad!' 'e shouted when I came up. Blimey! I couldn't stab 'im, so I took 'im prisoner. It's not 'arf a barney!... 'Ave yer got a fag ter spare?"

The Cockney came to a halt, reached for a cigarette, and lit it.

The German stood still, panting like a dog.

"Double! Fritz, double!" shouted the boy, sending a little puff of smoke through his nose. "Over to our trench you go! Grease along if yer don't want a bayonet in yer!"

They rushed off, the German with hands in air, and Bill behind with his bayonet perilously close to the prisoner. There was something amusing in the incident, and I could not refrain from laughing. Then I got a whiff from a German gas-bomb which exploded near me, and I began spluttering and coughing. The irritation, only momentary, was succeeded by a strange humour. I felt as if walking on air, my head got light, and it was with difficulty that I kept my feet on earth. It would be so easy to rise into space and float away.

The sensation was a delightful one; I felt so pleased with myself, with everything. A wounded man lay on the ground, clawing the earth with frenzied fingers. In a vague way, I remembered some ancient law which ordained me to assist a stricken man. But I could not do so now, the action would clog my buoyancy and that delightful feeling of freedom which permeated my being. Another soldier whom I recognised, even at a distance, by his pink-and-white bald pate, so often a subject for our jokes, reeled over the blood-stained earth, his eyes almost bursting from their sockets.

"You look bad," I said to him with a smile.

He stared at me drunkenly, but did not answer.

A man, mother-naked, raced round in a circle, laughing boisterously. The rags that would class him as a friend or foe were gone, and I could not tell whether he was an Englishman or a German. As I watched him an impartial bullet went through his forehead, and he fell headlong to the earth. The sight sobered me and I regained my normal self;

Up near the German wire I found our Company postman sitting in a shell-hole, a bullet in his leg below the knee, and an unlighted cigarette in his mouth.

"You're the man I want," he shouted, on seeing me. And I fumbled in my haversack for bandages.

"No dressing for me, yet," he said with a smile. "There are others needing help more than I. What I want is a match."

As I handed him my match box a big high explosive shell flew over our heads and dropped fifty yards away in a little hollow where seven or eight figures in khaki lay prostrate, faces to the ground. The shell burst and the wounded and dead rose slowly into air to a height of six or seven yards and dropped slowly again, looking for all the world like puppets worked by wires.

"This," said the postman, who had observed the incident, "is a solution of a question which diplomacy could not settle, I suppose. The last argument of kings is a damned sorry business."

By the German barbed wire entanglements were the shambles of war. Here our men were seen by the enemy for the first time that morning. Up till then the foe had fired erratically through the oncoming curtain of smoke; but when the cloud cleared away, the attackers were seen advancing, picking their way through the wires which had been cut to little pieces by our bombardment. The Irish were now met with harrying rifle fire, deadly petrol bombs and hand grenades. Here I came across dead, dying and sorely wounded; lives maimed and finished, and all the romance and roving that makes up the life of a soldier gone for ever. Here, too, I saw, bullet-riddled, against one of the spider webs known as *chevaux de frise,* a limp lump of pliable leather, the football which the boys had kicked across the field.

I came across Flannery lying close to a barbed wire support, one arm round it as if in embrace. He was a clumsily built fellow, with queer bushy eyebrows and a short, squat nose. His bearing was never soldierly, but on a march he could bear any burden and stick the job when more alert men fell out. He always bore himself however with a certain grace, due, perhaps, to a placid belief in his own strength. He never made friends; a being apart, he led a solitary life. Now he lay close to earth hugging an entanglement prop, and dying.

There was something savage in the expression of his face as he looked slowly round, like an ox under a yoke, on my approach. I knelt down beside him and cut his tunic with my scissors where a burnt hole clotted with blood showed under the kidney. A splinter of shell had torn part of the man's side away. All hope was lost for the poor soul.

"In much pain, chummy?" I asked.

"Ah, Chrfet! yes, Pat," he answered. "Wife and two kiddies, too. Are we getting the best of it?"

I did not know how the fight was progressing, but I had seen a line of bayonets drawing near to the second trench out by Loos.

"Winning all along," I answered.

"That's good," he said. "Is there any hope for me?"

"Of course there is, matey," I lied. "You have two of these morphia tablets and lie quiet. We'll take you in after a while, and you'll be back in England in two or three days' time."

I placed the morphia under his tongue and he closed his eyes as if going to sleep. Then, with an effort, he tried to get up and gripped the wire support with such vigour that it came clean out of the ground. His legs shot out from under him, and, muttering something about rations being fit for pigs and not for men, he fell back and died.

The fighting was not over in the front trench yet, the first two companies had gone ahead, the other two companies were taking possession here. A sturdy Bavarian in shirt and pants was standing on a banquette with his bayonet over the parapet, and a determined look in his eyes. He had already done for two of our men as they tried to cross, but now his rifle seemed to be unloaded and he waited. Standing there amidst his dead countrymen he formed a striking figure. A bullet from one of our rifles would have ended his career speedily, but no one seemed to want to fire that shot. There was a moment of suspense, broken only when the monstrous futility of resistance became apparent to him, and he threw down his rifle and put up his hands, shouting "Kamerad! kamerad!" I don't know what became of him afterwards, other events claimed my attention.

Four boys rushed up, panting under the machine gun and ammunition belts which they carried. One got hit and fell to the ground, the maxim tripod which he carried fell on top of him. The remainder of the party came to a halt.

"Lift the tripod and come along," his mates shouted to one another.

"Who's goin' to carry it?" asked a little fellow with a box of ammunition.

"You," came the answer.

"Some other one must carry it," said the little fellow. "I've the heaviest burden."

"You've not," one answered. "Get the blurry thing on your shoulder."

"Blurry yourself!" said the little fellow. "Someone else carry the thing. Marney can carry it."

"I'm not a damned fool!" said Marney. "It can stick there 'fore I take it across."

"Not much good goin' over without it," said the little fellow.

I left them there wrangling: the extra weight would have made no appreciable difference to any of them.

It was interesting to see how the events of the morning had changed the nature of the boys. Mild-mannered youths who had spent their working hours of civil life in scratching with inky pens on white paper, and their hours of relaxation in cutting capers on roller skates and helping dainty maidens to teas and ices, became possessed of mad Berserker rage and ungovernable fury. Now that their work was war the bloodstained bayonet gave them play in which they seemed to glory.

"Here's one that I've just done in," I heard M'Crone shout, looking approvingly at a dead German. "That's five of the bloody swine now."

M'Crone's mother never sends her son any money lest he gets into the evil habit of smoking cigarettes. He is of a religious turn of mind and delights in singing hymns, his favourite being, "There is a green hill far away." I never heard him swear before, but at Loos his language would make a navvy in a Saturday night taproom green with envy. M'Crone was not lacking in courage. I have seen him wait for death with untroubled front in a shell-harried trench, and now, inflicting pain on others, he was a fiend personified; such transformations are of common occurrence on the field of honour.

The German trench had suffered severely from our fire; parapets were blown in, and at places the trench was full to the level of the ground with sandbags and earth. Wreckage was strewn all over the place, rifles, twisted distortions of shapeless metal, caught by high-velocity shells, machine guns smashed to atoms, bombproof shelters broken to pieces like houses of cards; giants had been at work of destruction in a delicately fashioned nursery.

On the reverse slope of the parapet broken tins, rusty swords, muddy equipments, wicked-looking coils of barbed wire, and discarded articles of clothing were scattered about pell-mell. I noticed an unexploded shell perched on a sandbag, cocking a perky nose in air, and beside it was a battered helmet, the brass»glory of its regal eagle dimmed with trench mud and wrecked with many a bullet....

I had a clear personal impression of man's ingenuity for destruction when my eyes looked on the German front line where our dead lay in peace with their fallen enemies on the parapet. At the bottom of the trench the dead lay thick, and our boys, engaged in building a new parapet, were heaping the sandbags on the dead men and consolidating the captured position.

German, and I had spent seven months in France. At night when out on working-parties I saw figures moving out by the enemy trenches, mere shadows that came into view when an ephemeral constellation of star-shells held the heavens. We never fired at these shadows, and they never fired at us; it is unwise to break the tacit truces of the trenches. The first real live German I saw was the one who blundered down the ladder into 'our trench, the second raced towards our trenches with Bill Teake following at his heels, uttering threats and vowing that he would stab the prisoner if he did not double in a manner approved of by the most exacting sergeant-major.

Of those who are England'senemies I'know, even now, very little. I cannot well pass judgment on a nation through seeing distorted Jumps of clotting and mangled flesh pounded into the muddy floor of a trench, or strewn broadcast on the reverse slopes of a shell-scarred parapet. The enemy suffered as we did, yelled with pain when his wounds prompted him, forgot perhaps in the insane combat some of the nicer tenets of chivalry. After all, war is an approved licence for brotherly mutilation, its aims are sanctioned, only the means towards its end are disputed. It is a sad and sorry business from start to finish, from diplomacy that begets it to the Te Deums that rise to God in thanksgiving for victory obtained.

In the first German trench there were dozens of dead, the trench was literally piled with lifeless bodies in ugly grey uniforms. Curiosity prompted me to look into the famous German dug-outs. They were remarkable constructions, caves leading into the bowels of the earth, some of them capable of holding a whole platoon of soldiers. These big dug-outs had stairs leading down to the main chamber and steps leading out. In one I counted forty-seven steps leading down from the floor of the trench to the roof of the shelter. No shell made was capable of piercing these constructions, but a bomb flung downstairs...,.

I looked into a pretentious dug-out as I was going along the trench. This one, the floor of which was barely two feet below the level of the trench floor, must have been an officer's. It was sumptuously furnished, a curtained bed with a white coverlet stood in one corner. Near the door was a stove and a scuttle of coal. In another corner stood a table, and on it was a half bottle of wine, three glasses, a box of cigars, and a vase of flowers. These things I noticed later; what I saw first on entering was a wounded German lying across the bed, his head against the wall and his feet on the floor. His right arm was almost severed at the shoulder.

I entered and gazed at him. There was a look of mute appeal in his eyes, and for some reason I felt ashamed of myself for having intruded on the privacy of a dying man. There come times when a man on the field of battle should be left alone to his own thoughts. I unloosened my water-bottle from its holder and by sign inquired if he wanted a drink. He nodded, and I placed the bottle to his lips.

"Sprechen Anglais?" I inquired, and he shook his head.

I took my bottle of morphia tablets from my pocket and explained to him as well as I was able what the bottle contained, and he permitted me to place two under his tongue. When rummaging in my pocket I happened to bring out my rosary beads and he noticed them.

He spoke and I guessed that he was inquiring if I was a Catholic.

I nodded assent.

He fumbled with his left hand in his tunic pocket and brought out a little mudstained booklet and handed it to me. I noticed that the volume was a prayer-book. By his signs I concluded that he wanted me to keep it.

I turned to leave, but he called me back and pointed to his trousers pocket as if he wanted me to bring something out of it. I put in my hand and drew out a little leather packet from which the muzzle of a revolver peeped forth. This I put in my pocket. He feared that if some of our men found this in his possession his life might be a few hours shorter than it really would be if he were left to die in peace. J. could see that he required me to do something further for him. Raising his left hand with difficult (I now saw that blood was flowing down the wrist) he pointed at his tunic pocket, and I put my hand in there. A clasp-knife, a few buttons, a piece of string and a photo were all that the pocket contained. The photograph showed a man, whom I saw was the soldier, a woman and a little child seated at a table. I put it in his hand, and with brilliant eyes and set teeth he raised his head to look at it....

I went outside. M'Crone was coming along the trench with a bomb in his hand.

"Any of them in that dug-out?" he asked me.

"One," I replied.

"Then I'll give him this," M'Crone shouted. His gestures were violent, and his indifference to personal danger as shown in his loud laughter was somewhat exaggerated. As long as he had something to do he was all right, but a moment's thought would crumple him up like a wet rag.

"I've done in seven of them already," he shouted.

"The bne in here is dying," I said. "Leave him alone."

M'Crone went to the dug-out door, looked curiously in, then walked away.

Behind the German trench I found one of our boys slowly recovering from an attack of gas. Beside him lay a revolver, a mere toy of a thing, and touching him was a German with a bullet in his temple. The boy told me an interesting story as I propped him up in a sitting position against a couple of discarded equipments.

"I tripped up, and over I went," he said. "I came to slowly, and was conscious of many things 'fore I had the power to move my hands or feet. What do you think was happenin'? There was a bloomin' German sniper under cover pottin' at our boys, and that cover was a bundle of warm, livin' flesh; the blighter's cover was me! 'If I get my hand in my pocket,' I says to myself, 'I'll get my revolver and blow the beggar's brains out'"

"Blow out his brains with that!" I said, looking at the weapon. "You might as well try to blow out his brains with a pinch of snuff!"

"That's all you know!" said the boy. "Anyway, I got my hand into my pocket, it crawled in like a snake, and I got the little pet out. And the German was pot-pottin' all the time. Then I fetched the weapon up, stuck the muzzle plunk against the man's head and pulled the trigger twice. He didn't half kick up a row. See if the two bullets have gone through one hole, Pat."

"They have," I told him.

"I knew it," he answered. "Ah! it's an easy job to kill a man. You just rush at him and you see his eyes and nothin' else. There's a mist over the trench. You shove your bayonet forward and its sticks in something soft and almost gets dragged out of your hands. Then you get annoyed because you can't pull it back easy. That's all that happens and you've killed a man... , How much water have you got?"

A German youth of seventeen or eighteen with a magnificent helmet on his head and a red cross on his arm was working in the centre of a square formed by four of his dead countrymen, digging a grave. The sweat stood out on his forehead, and from time to time he cast an uneasy glance about him.

"What are you doing there?" I asked.

"Digging a grave for these," he said, in good English, pointing a shaky finger at the prostrate figures. "I suppose I'll be put in it myself," he added.

"Why?" I inquired.

"Oh! you English shoot all prisoners."

"You're a fool, Fritz," said M'Crone, approaching him. "We're not going to do you any harm. Look, I've brought you something to eat."

He handed the boy a piece of cake, but the young Bavarian shook his head. He was trembling with terror, and the shovel shook in his hands. Fifteen minutes later when I passed that way carrying in a wounded man, I saw M'Crone and the young Bavarian sitting on the brink of the grave smoking cigarettes and laughing heartily over some joke.

Prisoners were going down towards M across the open. Prisoners are always taken across the open in bulk with as small an escort as possible. I saw a mob of two hundred go along, their hands in the air, and stern Tommies marching on flank and at rear. The party was a mixed one. Some of the prisoners were strong, sturdy youngsters of nineteen or twenty, others were old men, war-weary and dejected. A few were thin, weedy creatures, but others were massive blocks of bone and muscle, well set-up and brimful of energy even in their degrading plight.

Now and again queer assortments of these came along. One man was taken prisoner in a cellar on the outskirts of Loos. Our men discovered him asleep in a bed, pulled him out and found that he was enjoying a decent, civilised slumber. He came down to M as he was taken prisoner, his sole clothing being a pair of stockings, a shirt and an identity disc. Four big Highlanders, massive of shoulder and leg, escorted a puny, spectacled youth along the rim of the trench, and following them came a diminutive Cockney with a massive helmet on his head, the sole escort for twelve gigantic Bavarian Grenadiers. The Cockney had now only one enemy, he was the man who offered to help him at his work.

I came across a crumpled figure of a man in grey, dead in a shell-crater. One arm was bent under him, the other stretched forward almost touching a photograph of a woman and three little children. I placed the photograph under the edge of the man's tunic.

Near him lay another Bavarian, an old man, deeply wrinkled and white haired, and wounded through the chest. He was trembling all over like a wounded bird, but his eyes were calm and they looked beyond the tumult and turmoil of the battlefield into some secret world that only the dying can see. A rosary was in the man's hand and his lips were mumbling something: he. was telling his beads. He took no notice of me. Across the level at this point came a large party of prisoners amidst a storm of shells. The German gunners had shortened their range and were now shelling the ground occupied by their troops an hour previous. Callous, indifferent destruction! The oncoming prisoners were Germans—as men they were of no use to us; it would cost our country money and men to keep and feed them. They were Germans, but of no further use to Germany; they were her pawns in a game of war and now useless in the play. As if to illustrate this, a shell from a German gun dropped in the midst of the batch and pieces of the abject party whirled in air. The gun which had destroyed them had acted as their guardian for months. It was a frantic mother slaying her helpless brood.

The stretcher-bearer sees all the horror of war written in blood and tears on the shell-riven battlefield. The wounded man, thank heaven! has only his own pain to endure, although the most extreme agony which flesh is heir to is written large on the field of fight.

Several times that day I asked myself the question, "Why are all soldiers not allowed to carry morphia?" How much pain it would save! How many pangs of pain might morphia alleviate! How often would it give that rest and quiet which a man requires when an excited heart persists in pumping blood out through an open wound! In the East morphia is known as "The gift of God"; on the field of battle the gift of God should not be denied to men in great pain. It would be well indeed if all soldiers were taught first aid before a sergeant-major teaches them the art of forming fours on the parade ground.

v CHAPTER VIII HOW MY COMRADES FARED

Seven supple lads and clean Sat down to drink one night,
Sat down to drink at Nouex-les-Mines-,
  Then went away to fight.
Seven supple lads and clean Are finished with the fight;
But only three at Nouex-les-Mines
  Sit down to drink to-night.

FELAN went up the ladder of the assembly trench with a lighted cigarette in his mouth. Out on the open his first feeling was one of disappointment; to start with, the charge was as dull as a church parade. Felan, although orders were given to the contrary, expected a wild, whooping forward rush, but the men stepped out soberly, with the pious decision of ancient ladies going to church. In front the curtain of smoke receded, but the air stunk with its pungent odour still. A little valley formed by the caprice of the breeze opened in the fumes and its far end disclosed the enemy's wire entanglements. Felan walked through the valley for a distance of five yards, then he glanced to his right and found that there was nobody in sight there. Pryor had disappeared.

"Here, Bill, we've lost connection!" he cried, turning to his left. But his words were wasted on air; he was alone in his little glen, and invisible birds flicked angry wings close to his ears. His first inclination was to turn back, not through fear, but with a desire to make inquiries.

"I can't take a trench by myself," he muttered. "Shall I go back? If I do so some may call me a coward. Oh, damn it! I'll go forward."

He felt afraid now, but his fear was not that which makes a man run away; he was attracted towards that which engendered the fear as an urchin attracted towards a wasps' nest longs to poke the hive and annoy its occupants.

"Suppose I get killed now and see nothing," he said to himself. "Where is Bill, and Pryor, and the others?"

He reached the enemy's wire, tripped, and fell headlong. He got to his feet again and took stock of the space in front. There was the German trench, sure enough, with its rows of dirty sandbags, a machine-gun emplacement and a maxim peeping furtively through the loophole. A big, bearded German was adjusting the range of the weapon. He looked at Felan, Felan looked at him and tightened his grip on his rifle.

"You!" said Felan, and just made one step forward when something "hit him all over," as he said afterwards. He dropped out of the world of conscious things.

A stretcher-bearer found him some twenty minutes later and placed him in a shell-hole, after removing his equipment, which he placed on the rim of the crater.

Felan returned to a conscious life that was tense with agony. Pain gripped at the innermost parts of his being. "I cannot stand this," he yelled. "God Almighty, it's hell!"

He felt as if somebody was shoving a red-hot bar of iron through his chest. Unable to move, he lay still, feeling the bar getting shoved further and further in. For a moment he had a glimpse of his rifle lying on the ground near him and he tried to reach it. But the unsuccessful effort cost him much, and he became unconscious again.

A shell bursting near his hand shook him into reality, and splinters whizzed by his head. He raised himself upwards, hoping to get killed outright. He was unsuccessful. Again his eyes rested on his rifle.

"If God would give me strength to get it into my hand," he muttered. "Lying here like a rat in a trap and I've seen nothing. Not a run for my money.... I suppose all the boys are dead. Lucky fellows if they die easy.... I've seen nothing only one German, and he done for me. I wish the bullet had gone through my head."

He looked at his equipment, at the bayonet scabbard lying limply under the haversack. The water-bottle hung over the rim of the shell-hole. "Full of rum, the bottle is, and I'm so dry. I wish I could get hold of it. I was a damned fool ever to join the Army.... My God! I wish I was dead," said Felan.

The minutes passed by like a long grey thread unwinding itself slowly from some invisible ball, and the pain bit deeper into the boy. Vivid remembrances of long-past events flashed across his mind and fled away like telegraph poles seen by passengers in an express train. Then he lost consciousness again.

About eleven o'clock in the morning I found a stretcher-bearer whose mate had been wounded, and he helped me to carry a wounded man into our original front trench. On our way across I heard somebody calling "Pat! Pat!" I looked round and saw a man crawling in on his hands and knees, his head almost touching the ground. He called to me, but he did not look in my direction. But I recognised the voice: the corporal was calling. I went across to him.

"Wounded?" I asked.

"Yes, Pat," he answered, and, turning, over, he sat down. His face was very, white.

"You should not have crawled in," I muttered. "It's only wearing you out; and it's not very healthy here."

"Oh, I wanted to get away from this hell," he said.

"It's very foolish," I replied. "Let me see your wound."

I dressed the wound and gave the corporal two morphia tablets and put two blue crosses on his face. This would tell those who might come his way later that morphia had been given.

"Lie down," I said. "When the man whom we're carrying is safely in, we'll come back for you."

I left him. In the trench were many wounded lying on the floor and on the fire-steps. A soldier was lying face downwards, groaning. A muddy ground-sheet was placed over his shoulders. I raised the sheet and found that his wound was not dressed.

"Painful, matey?" I asked.

"Oh, it's old Pat," muttered the man.

"Who are you?" I asked, for I did not recognise the voice.

"You don't know me!" said the man, surprise in his tones.

He turned a queer, puckered face half round, but I did not recognise him even then; pain had so distorted his countenance.

"No," I replied. "Who are you?"

"Felan," he replied.

"My God!" I cried, then hurriedly, "I'll dress your wound. You'll get carried in to the dressing-station directly."

"It's about time," said Felan wearily. "I've been out a couple of days.... Is there no R.A.M.C.?"

I dressed Felan's wound, returned, and looked for the corporal, but I could not find him. Someone must have carried him in, I thought.

Kore had got to the German barbed-wire entanglement when he breathed in a mouthful of smoke which almost choked him at first, and afterwards instilled him with a certain placid confidence in everything. He came to a leisurely halt and looked around him. In front, a platoon of the 20th London Regiment, losing its objective, crossed parallel to the enemy's trench. Then he saw a youth who was with him at school, and he shouted to him. The youth stopped; Kore came up and the boys shook hands, leant on their rifles, and began to talk of old times when a machine gun played about their ears. Both got hit.

M'Crone disappeared; he was never seen by any of his regiment after the 25th.

The four men were reported as killed in the casualty list.

CHAPTER IX AT LOOS

"The wages of sin and a soldier is death."—Trench Proverb. FOR long I had looked on Loos from a distance, had seen the red-brick houses huddled together brooding under the shade of the massive Twin Towers, the giant sentinels of the German stronghold. Between me and the village lurked a thousand rifles and death-dealing maxims; out in the open no understanding could preserve a man from annihilation, luck alone could save him.

On September 25th I lived in the village. By night a ruined village has a certain character of its own, the demolition of war seems to give each broken wall a consciousness of dignity and worth; the moonlight ripples over the chimneys, and sheaves of shadow lurk in every nook and corner. But by day, with its broken, jerry-built houses, the village has no relieving features, it is merely a heap of broken bricks, rubble and mud. Some day, when ivy and lichen grow up the walls and cover green the litter that was Loos, a quaint, historical air may be given to the scene, but now it showed nothing but a depressing sameness of latchless doors, hingeless shutters, destruction and decay. Gone was all the fascinating, pathetic melancholy of the night when we took possession, but such might be expected: the dead is out of keeping with the day.

I was deep in thought as I stood at the door of the dressing-station, the first in Loos, and at the moment, the only one. The second German trench, the trench that was the enemy's at dawn, ran across the bottom of the street, and our boys were busy there heaping sandbags on the parapet. A dozen men with loaded rifles stood in the dressing-station on guard, and watchful eyes scanned the streets, looking for the enemy who were still in hiding in the cellars or sniping from the upper stories of houses untouched by shellfire. Down in our cellar the wounded and dying lay: by night, if they lived till then, we would carry them across the open to the dressing-station of Maroc. To venture across now, when the big guns chorused a fanfare of fury on the levels, would have been madness.

I went to the door and looked up the street; it was totally deserted; a dead mule and several khaki-clad figures lay on the pavement, and vicious bullets kicked up showers of sparks on the cobblestones. I could not tell where they were fired from.... A voice called my name and I turned round to see a head peep over the trench where it crossed the road. My mate, Bill Teake, was speaking.

"Come 'ere!" he called. "There's some doin's goin' to take place."

I rushed across the open road where a machine gun from a hill on the right was sending its messages with shrewish persistence, and tumbled into the trench at my mate's side.

"What are the doings?" I asked.

"The word 'as been passed along that a German observation balloon is going up over Lens an' we're goin' to shell it," said Bill.

"I can't see the blurry thing nohow," he added.

I looked towards Lens, and saw the town pencilled reddish in the morning light with several defiant chimney stacks standing in air. One of these was smoking, which showed that the enemy was still working it.

I saw the balloon rise over the town. It was a massive banana-like construction with ends pointing downwards, and it climbed slowly up the heavens. At that moment our gunners greeted it with a salvo of shrapnel and struck it, as far as I could judge.

It wriggled for a moment, like a big feather caught in a drift of air, then disappeared with startling suddenness.

"A neat shot," I said to Bill, who was now engaged on the task of looking for the snappy maxim shrew that tapped impatiently on the sandbagged parapet.

"I think it's up there," he said, pointing to the crest where three or four red-tiled houses snuggled in the cover of a spinney. "It's in one of them big 'ouses, bet yer. If I find it I'll get the artillery to blow the place to blazes!" he concluded, with an air of finality.

I went back to the dressing-station and found the men on guard in a state of tense excitement. They had seen a German cross the street two hundred yards up, and a red-haired youth, Ginger Turley, who had fired at the man, vowed that he had hit him.

"I saw 'im fall," said Ginger. "Then 'e crawled into a 'ouse on 'ands and knees."

"'E was only shammin'," said the corporal of the guard. "Nobody can be up to these 'ere Allemongs."

"I 'it 'im," said Ginger heatedly. "Couldn't miss a man at two 'undred and me gettin' proficiency pay for good shootin' at S'nalbans (St. Albans)."

A man at the door suddenly uttered a loud yell.

"Get yer 'ipes," he yelled. "Quick! Grease out of it and get into the scrap. There's 'undreds of 'em up the streets. Come on! Come out of it! We'll give the swine socks!"

He rushed into the street, raised his rifle to his shoulder and fired two rounds. Then he raced up the street shouting, with the guard following. I looked out.

The men in khaki were rushing on a mob of some fifty or sixty Germans who advanced to meet them with trembling arms raised over their heads, signifying in their manner that they wished to surrender. I had seen many Germans surrender that morning and always noticed that their uplifted arms shook as if stricken with palsy. I suppose they feared what might befall them when they fell into our hands.

With hands still in air and escorted by our boys they filed past the door of the dressing-station. All but one man, who was wounded in the jaw.

"This is a case for you, Pat," said the corporal of the guard, and beckoned to the wounded German to come indoors.

He was an ungainly man, and his clothes clung to his body like rags to a scarecrow. His tunic was ripped in several places, and a mountain of Loos mud clung to his trousers. His face was an interesting one, his eyes, blue and frank, seemed full of preoccupation that put death out of reckoning.

"Sprechen Anglais?" I asked, floundering in the mud of Franco-Germaine interrogation. He shook his head; the bullet had blown away part of the man's jaw and he could not speak.

I dressed his wound in silence, an ugly, ghastly wound it looked, one that he would hardly recover from. As I worked with the bandages he brought out a little mirror, gazed for a moment at his face in the glass, and shook his head sadly. He put the mirror back in his pocket, but after a second he drew it out again and made a second inspection of his wound.

The dressing done, I inquired by signs if he wanted to sleep; there was still some room in the cellar. He pointed his finger at his tunic over the breast and I saw a hole there that looked as if made by a red-hot poker. I cut the clothes off the man with my scissors and discovered that the bullet which went through the man's jaw had also gone through his chest. He was bleeding freely at the back near the spine and in front over the heart.... The man brought out his mirror again, and, standing with his back to a shattered looking-glass that still remained in the building, he examined his wound after the manner of a barber who shows his customer the back of his head by use of a mirror.... Again the German shook his head sadly. I felt sorry for the man. My stock of bandages had run short, and Ginger Turley, who had received a parcel of underclothing a few days before, brought out a new shirt from fiis haversack, and tearing it into strips, he handed me sufficient cloth for a bandage.

"Poor bloke!" muttered Turley, blushing a little as if ashamed of the kind action. "I suppose it was my shot, too. 'E must be the feller that went crawlin' into the buildin'."

"Not necessarily," I said, hoping to comfort Ginger.

"It was my shot that did it, sure enough," Ginger persisted. "I couldn't miss at two 'undred yards, not if I tried."

One of the men was looking at a little book, somewhat similar to the pay-book we carry on active service, which fell from the German's pocket.

"Bavarian!" read the man with the book, and fixed a look of interrogation on the wounded man, who nodded.

"Musician?" asked the man, who divined that certain German words stated that the Bavarian was a musician in civil life.

A sad look crept into the prisoner's eyes. He raised his hands and held them a little distance from his lips and moved his fingers rapidly; then he curved his left arm and drew his right slowly backward and forward across in front of his body.

We understood; he played the flute and violin. Ginger Turley loves ragtime and is a master of the mouth-organ; and now having met a brother artist in such a woeful plight, Ginger's feelings overcame him, and two tears gathered in his eyes.

"I wish I wasn't such a good shot," he muttered.

We wrapped the German up in a few rags, and since he wanted to follow his comrades, who left under escort, we allowed him to go. Ten minutes later, Bill Teake poked his little white potato of a nose round the door.

"I've found 'im out," he said, and his voice was full of enthusiasm.

"Who have you found out?" I asked.

"That bloomin' machine gun," Bill answered. "I saw a little puff of smoke at one of the winders of a 'ouse up in the spinney. I kept my eye on that 'ere winder. Ev'ry time I seed a puff of smoke, over comes a bullet. I told the officer, and he 'phones down to the artillery. There's goin' to be some doin's. Come on, Pat, and see the fun."

It was too good to miss. Both of us scurried across the road and took up a position in the trench from which we could get a good view of the spinney.

"That 'ouse there," said Bill, pointing to the red-brick building bordering a slag-heap known as "The Double Crassier" which tailed to a thin point near the village of Maroc. "There! see at the winder on the left a puff of smoke."

A bullet hit the sandbag at my side. I looked at the house indicated by Bill and saw a wisp of pale smoke trail up from one of the lower windows towards the roof.

"The machine gun's there, sure enough," I said.

Then a bigger gun spoke; a shell whizzed through the air and raised a cloud of black dust from the rim of the slag-heap.

"More to the left, you bounders, more to the left!" yelled Bill.

He could not have been more intent on the work if he were the gunner engaged upon the task of demolition.

The second shot crept nearer and a shrub uprooted whirled in air.

"That's the ticket!" yelled Bill, clapping his hands. "Come, gunner, get the bounder next time!"

The gunner got him with the next shot which struck the building fair in the centre and smashed it to pieces.

"That was a damned good one," said Bill approvingly. "The bloomin' gun is out of action now for the duration of war. Have you seen that bloke?"

Bill Teake pointed at a dead German who lay on the crest of the parados, his hands doubled under him, and his jaw bound with a bloodstained dressing.

"He just got killed a minute ago," said Bill. "He jumped across the trench when the machine gun copped 'im an 'e went down flop!"

"I've just dressed his wounds," I said.

"He'll need no dressin' now," said Bill, and added compassionately, "Poor devil! S'pose 'e 's 'ad some one as cared for 'im."

I thought of home and hoped to send a letter along to Maroc with a wounded man presently. From there letters would be forwarded. I had a lead pencil in my pocket, but I had no envelope.

"I'll give you a half-franc for a green envelope," I said, and Bill Teake took from his pocket the green envelope, which needed no regimental censure, but was liable to examination at the Base.

"'Arf-franc and five fags," he said, speaking with the studied indifference of a fishwife making a bargain.

"Half a franc and two fags," I answered.

"'Arf a franc and four fags," he said.

"Three fags," I ventured.

"Done," said Bill, and added, "I've now sold the bloomin' line of communication between myself and my ole man for a few coppers and three meesly fags."

"What's your old man's profession, Bill?" I asked.

"'Is wot?"

"His trade?"

"Yer don't know my ole man, Pat?" he inquired. "Everybody knows 'im. 'E 'as as good a reputation as old Times. Yer must 'ave seen 'im in the Strand wiv 'is shiny buttons, burnished like gold in a jooler's winder, carryin' a board wiv 'Globe Metal Polish' on it."

"Oh!" I said with a laugh.

"But 'e's a devil for 'is suds 'e is"

"What are suds?" I asked.

"Beer," said Bill. "'E can 'old more'n any man in Lunnon, more'n the chucker-out at 'The

Cat and Mustard Pot' boozer in W Road even. Yer should see the chucker-out an' my ole man comin' 'ome on Saturday night. They keep themselves steady by rollin' in opposite directions."

"Men with good reputations don't roll home inebriated," I said. "Excessive alcoholic dissipation is utterly repugnant to dignified humanity."

"Wot!"

"Is your father a churchgoer?" I asked.

"Not 'im," said Bill. "'E don't believe that one can go to 'eaven by climbin' up a church steeple. 'E's a good man, that's wot 'e is. 'E works 'ard when 'e's workin', 'e can use 'is fives wiv anyone, 'e can take a drink or leave it, but 'e prefers takin' it. Nobody can take a rise out o' 'im fer 'e knows 'is place, an' that's more'n some people do."

"Bill, did you kill any Germans this morning?" I asked.

"Maybe I did," Bill answered, "and maybe I didn't. I saw one bloke, an Allemong, in the front trench laughin' like 'ell. Til make yer laugh,' I said to 'im, and shoved my bayonet at 'is bread basket. Then I seed 'is foot; it was right off at the ankle. I left 'im alone. After that I 'ad a barney. I was goin' round a traverse and right in front of me was a Boche, eight foot 'igh or more. Oh! 'e 'ad a bayonet as long as 'imself, and a beard as long as 'is bayonet."

"What did you do?"

"Oh! I retreated," said Bill. "Then I met four of the Jocks, they 'ad bombs. I told them wot I seen an' they went up with me to the place. The Boche saw us and 'e rushed inter a dug-out. One of the Jocks threw a bomb, and bang!"

"Have you seen Kore?" I asked.

"No, I didn't see 'im at all," Bill answered. "I was mad for a while. Then I saw a lot of Alleymongs rush into a dug-out. 'Gor-blimey!'

I said to the Jocks, 'we'll give 'em 'ell,' and I caught 'old of a German bomb, one 'o them kind where you pull the string out and this sets the fuse goin'. I coiled the string round my fingers and pulled. But I couldn't loosen the string. It was a go! I 'eld out my arm with the bomb 'angin'. 'Take it off!' I yelled to the Jocks. Yer should see them run off. There was no good in me runnin'. Blimey! I didn't 'arf feel bad. Talk about a cold sweat; I sweated icicles! And there was the damned bomb 'angin' from my 'and and me thinkin' it was goin' to burst. But it didn't; I 'adn't pulled the string out far enough.

"And that's Loos," he went on, standing on the fire-step and looking up the road. "It's bashed about a lot. There's 'ardly a 'ouse standin'. And that's the Tower Bridge," he added, looking fixedly at the Twin Towers that stood scarred but unbroken over Loos coal mine.

"There was a sniper up there this mornin'," he told me. "'E didn't 'arf cause some trouble. Knocked out dozens of our fellers. 'E was brought down at last by a bomb."

He laughed as he spoke, then became silent. For fully five minutes there was not a word spoken.

I approached the parapet stealthily and looked up the street of Loos, a solemn, shell-scarred, mysterious street where the dead lay amidst the broken tiles. Were all those brown bundles dead men? Some of them maybe were still dying; clutching at life with vicious energy. A bundle lay near me, a soldier in khaki with his hat gone. I could see his close, compact, shiny curls which seemed to have been glued on to his skull. Clambering up the parapet I reached forward and turned him round and saw his face. It was leaden-hued and dull; the wan and almost colourless eyes fixed on me in a vague and glassy stare, the jaw dropped sullenly, and the tongue hung out. Dead.... And up the street, down in the cellars, at the base of the Twin Towers, they were dying. How futile it was to trouble about one when thousands needed help. Where should I begin? Who should I help first? Any help I might be able to give seemed so useless. I had been at work all the morning dressing the wounded, but there were so many. I was a mere child emptying the sea with a tablespoon. I crawled into the trench again to find Bill still looking over the parapet. This annoyed me. Why, I could not tell.

"What are you looking at?" I asked.

There was no answer. I looked along the trench and saw that all the men were looking towards the enemy's line; watching, as it seemed, for something to take place. None knew what the next moment would bring forth. The expectant mood was prevalent. All were waiting.

Up the road some houses were still peopled with Germans, and snipers were potting at us with malicious persistency, but behind the parapet we were practically immune from danger. As we looked a soldier appeared round the bend of the trench, the light of battle in his eyes and his body festooned with bombsi

"It's dangerous to go up the centre of the street," I called to him as he came to a halt beside me and looked up the village.

"Bend down," I said. "Your head is over the parapet." I recognised the man. He was Gilhooley the bomber.

"What does it matter?" he muttered. "I want to get at them.... Oh! I know yer face.... D'ye mind the champagne at Nouex-les-Mines.... These bombs are real ones, me boy.... Do you know where the snipers are?"

"There's one up there," I said, raising my head and pointing to a large house on the left of the road near the Twin Towers. "I saw the smoke of his rifle when he fired at me a while ago."

"Then he must get what he's lookin' for," said Gilhooley, tightening his belt of bombs, and, clutching his rifle, rushed out into the roadway. "By Jasus! I'll get him out of it!"

I raised my head and watched, fascinated. With prodigious strides Gilhooley raced up the street, his rifle clutched tightly in his hand. Suddenly he paused, as if in thought, and his rifle went clattering across the cobbles. Then he sank slowly to the ground, kicking out a little with his legs. The bullet had hit him in the jaw and it came out through the back of his neck....

I could hear the wounded crying and moaning somewhere near, or perhaps far away. A low, lazy breeze slouched up from the field which we had crossed that morning, and sound travelled far. The enemy snipers on Hulluch copse were busy, and probably the dying were being hit again. Some of them desired it, the slow process of dying on the open field of war is so dreadful.... A den of guns, somewhere near Lens, became voluble, and a monstrous fanfare of fury echoed in the heavens. The livid sky seemed to pull itself up as if to be out of the way; under it the cavalcades of war ran riot. A chorus of screeches and yells rose trembling and whirling in air, snatching at each other like the snarling and barking of angry dogs.

Bill stood motionless, looking at the enemy's line, his gaze concentrated on a single point; in his eyes there was a tense, troubled expression, as if he was calculating a sum which he could not get right. Now and again he would shake his head as if trying to throw something off and address a remark to the man next him, who did not seem to hear. Probably he was asleep. In the midst of artillery tumult some men are overcome with languor and drop asleep as they stand. On the other hand, many get excited, burst into song and laugh boisterously at most commonplace incidents.

Amidst the riot, an undertone of pain became more persistent than ever. The levels where the wounded lay were raked with shrapnel that burst viciously in air and struck the bloodstained earth with spiteful vigour.

The cry for stretcher-bearers came down the trench, and I hurried off to attend to the stricken. I met him crawling along on all fours, looking like an ungainly lobster that has escaped from a basket. A bullet had hit the man in the back and he was in great pain; so much in pain that when I was binding his wound he raised his fist and hit me in the face.

"I'm sorry," he muttered, a moment afterwards. "I didn't mean it, but, my God! this is hell!"

"You'll have to lie here," I said, when I put the bandage on. "You'll get carried out at night when we can cross the open."

"I'm going now," he said. "I want to go now. I must get away. You'll let me go, won't you, Pat?"

"You'll be killed before you're ten yards across the open," I said. "Better wait till to-night."

"Does the trench lead out?" he asked.

"It probably leads to the front trench which the Germans occupied this morning," I said.

"Well, if we get there it will be a step nearer the dressing-station, anyway," said the wounded boy. "Take me away from here, do please."

"Can you stand upright?"

"I'll try," he answered, and half weeping and half laughing, he got to his feet. "I'll be able to walk down," he muttered.

We set off. I walked in front, urging the men ahead to make way for a wounded man. No order meets with such quick obedience as "Make way for wounded."

All the way from Loos to the churchyard which the trench fringes and where the bones of the dead stick out through the parapet, the trench was in fairly good order, beyond that was the dumping ground of death.

The enemy in their endeavour to escape from the Irish that morning crowded the trench like sheep in a lane-way, and it was here that the bayonet, rifle-butt and bomb found them. Now they lay six deep in places.... One bare-headed man lay across the parapet, his hand grasping his rifle, his face torn to shreds with rifle bullets. One of his own countrymen, hidden in Hulluch copse, was still sniping at the dead thing, believing it to be an English soldier. Such is the irony of war. The wounded man ambled painfully behind me, grunting and groaning. Sometimes he stopped for a moment, leant against the side of the trench and swore for several seconds. Then he muttered a word of apology and followed me in silence. When we came to the places where the dead lay six deep we had to crawl across them on our hands and knees. To raise our heads over the parapet would be courting quick death. We would become part of that demolition of blood and flesh that was necessary for our victory. In front of us a crowd of civilians, old men, women and children, was crawling and stumbling over the dead bodies. A little boy was eating the contents of a bully-beef tin with great relish, and the ancient female who accompanied him crossed herself whenever she stumbled across a prostrate German. The civilians were leaving Loos.

On either side we could hear the wounded making moan, their cry was like the yelping of drowning puppies. But the man who was with me seemed unconscious of his surroundings; seldom even did he notice the dead on the floor of the trench; he walked over them unconcernedly.

I managed to bring him down to the dressingstation. When we arrived he sat on a seat and cried like a child. CHAPTER X

A NIGHT IN LOOS

"Never see good in an enemy until you have defeated him."—War Proverb.
WILIGHT softened the gaunt corners of the ruined houses, and sheaves of shadows cowered in unfathomable corners. A wine shop, gashed and fractured, said "hush!" to us as we passed; the shell-holed streets gaped at the indifferent, unconcerned sky.

"See the streets are yawning," I said to my mate, Bill Teake.

"That's because they're bored," he replied.

"Bill," I said, "what do you mean by bored?"

"They've holes in them," he answer. "Why d'yer arst me?"

"I wanted to know if you were trying to make a pun," I said. "That's all."

Bill grunted, and a moment's silence ensued.

"Suppose it were made known to you, Bill," I said, "that for the rest of your natural life this was all you could look forward to, dull hours of waiting in the trenches, sleep in sodden dugouts, eternal gun-firing and innumerable bayonetcharges; what would you do?"

"Wot would I do?" said Bill, coming to a halt in the middle of the street. "This is wot I'd do," he said with decision. "I'd put a round in the breech, lay my 'ead on the muzzle of my 'ipe, and reach down and pull the blurry trigger. Wot would you do?"

"I should become very brave," I replied.

"I see wot yer mean," said Bill. "Ye'd be up to the Victoria Cross caper, and run yer nose into danger every time yer got a chance."

"You may be right," I replied. "No one likes this job, but we all endure it as a means towards an end."

"Flat!" I yelled, flopping to the ground and dragging Bill with me, as a shell burst on a house up the street and flung a thousand splinters round our heads. For a few seconds we cowered in the mud, then rose to our feet again.

"There are means by which we are going to end war," I said. "Did you see the dead and wounded to-day, the men groaning and shrieking, the bombs flung down into cellars, the blood-stained bayonets, the gouging and the gruelling; all those things are means towards creating peace in a disordered world.

The unrest which precedes night made itself felt in Loos. Crows made their way homeward, cleaving the air with weary wings; a tottering wall fell on the street with a melancholy clatter, and a joist creaked near at hand, yearning, as it seemed, to break free from its shattered neighbours. A lone wind rustled down the street, weeping over the fallen bricks, and crooning across barricades and machine-gun emplacements. The greyish-white evening sky cast a vivid pallor over the Twin Towers, which stood out sharply defined against the lurid glow of a fire in Lens.

All around Loos lay the world of trenches, secret streets, sepulchral towns, houses whose chimneys scarcely reached the level of the earth, crooked alleys, bayonet circled squares, and lonely graveyards where dead soldiers lay in the silent sleep that wakens to no earthly reveille.

The night fell. The world behind the German lines was lighted up with a white glow, the clouds seemed afire, and ran with a flame that was not red and had no glare. The tint was pale, and it trailed over Lens and the spinneys near the town, and spread trembling over the levels. White as a winding sheet, it looked like a fire of frost, vast and wide diffused. Every object in Loos seemed to loose its reality, a spectral glimmer hung over the ruins, and the walls were no more than outlines. The Twin Towers was a tracery of silver and enchanted fairy construction that the sun at dawn might melt away, the barbed-wire entanglements (those in front of the second German trench had not been touched by our artillery) were fancies in gossamer. The world was an enchanted poem of contrasts of shadow and shine, of nooks and corners black as ebony, and prominent objects that shone with a spiritual glow. Men coming down the street bearing stretchers or carrying rations were phantoms, the men stooping low over the earth digging holes for their dead comrades were as ghostly as that which they buried. I lived in a strange world—a world of dreams and illusions.

Where am I? I asked myself. Am I here? Do I exist? Where are the boys who marched with me from Les Brebis last night? I had looked on them during the day, seeing them as I had never seen them before, lying in silent and unquestioning peace, close to the yearning earth. Never again should I hear them sing in the musty barns near Givenchy; never again would we drink red wine together in Cafe Pierre le Blanc, Nouexles-Mines....

Bill Teake went back to his duties in the trench and left me.

A soldier came down the street and halted opposite.

"What's that light, soldier?" he asked me.

"I'm sure I don't know," I answered.

"I hear it's an ammunition depot afire in Lens," said the man. "Our shells hit it, and their blurry bullets have copped me now," he muttered, dropping on the roadway and crawling towards the shelter of the wall on his belly.

"Where are you hit?" I asked, helping him into the ruins of the *estaminet*—my dressing-station.

"In the leg," he answered, "just below the knee. It was when I was speaking to you about the ammunition depot on fire. 'Our shells hit it,' I said, and just then something went siss! through my calf. 'Their blurry bullets have copped me now,' I said, didn't I?"

"You did," I answered, laying my electric torch on the table and placing the wounded man on the floor. I ripped open his trousers and found the wound; the bullet had gone through the calf.

"Can you use your foot?" I asked, and he moved his boot up and down.

"No fracture," I told him. "You're all right for blighty, matey."

One of my mates who was sleeping in a cellar came up at that moment.

"Still dressing wounded, Pat?" he asked.

"I just got wounded a minute ago," said the man on the floor as I fumbled about with a first field dressing. "I was speaking to Pat about the fire at Lens, and I told him that our shells hit it, 'and a blurry bullet has copped me now,' I said, when I felt something go siss! through my leg."

"Lucky dog," said the man on the stair head. "I'd give fifteen pounds for your wound."

"Nothing doing," said the man on the floor with a laugh.

"When can I get down to the dressing-station?" he asked.

"Now, if you can walk," I told him. "If you're to be carried I shall need three other men; the mud is knee deep on the road to Maroc."

"I'll see if I can walk," said the man, and tried to rise to his feet. The effort was futile, he collapsed like a wet rag. Fifteen minutes later four of us left Loos bearing a stretcher on our shoulders, and trudged across the fields to the main road and into the crush of war traffic, hideously incongruous in the pale light of the quiet night. The night was quiet, for sounds that might make for riot were muffled by the mud. The limbers' wheels were mud to the axles, the mules drew their legs slowly out of muck almost reaching their bellies. Motor ambulances, wheeled stretchers, ammunition wagons, gun carriages, limbers, water-carts, mules, horses and men going up dragged their sluggish way through the mud on one side of the road; mules, horses and men, water-carts, limbers, gun carriages, ammunition wagons, wheeled stretchers and motor ambulances coming down moved slowly along the other side. Every man had that calm and assured indifference that comes with ordinary everyday life. Each was full of his own work, preoccupied with his toil, he was lost to the world around him. For the driver of the cart that we followed, a problem had to be worked out. The problem was this: how could he bring his mules and vehicles into Maroc and bring up a second load, then pilot his animals through mud and fire into Les Brebis before dawn; feed himself and his mules (when he got into safety), drink a glass or two of wine (if he had the money to pay for it), and wrap himself in his blanket and get to sleep in decent time for a good day's rest. Thus would he finish his night of work if the gods were kind. But they were not.

A momentary stoppage, and the mules stood stiffly in the mud, the off-side wheeler twitching a long, restless ear. The driver lay back in his seat, resigned to the delay. I could see his whip in air, his face turned to the east where the blazing star-shells lit the line of battle. A machine gun spoke from Hill 70, and a dozen searching bullets whizzed about our heads. The driver uttered a sharp, infantile yell like a snared rabbit, leant sideways, and fell down on the roadway. The mule with the twitching ear dropped on top of the man and kicked out wildly with its hind legs.

"Cut the 'oss out!" yelled someone from the top of a neighbouring wagon, and three or four soldiers rushed to the rescue, pulled the driver clear, and felt his heart.

"Dead," one said, dodging to avoid the hoofs of the wounded mule. "The bullet 'as caught the poor cove in the forehead.... Well, it's all over now, and there's nothing to be done."

"Shoot the mule," someone suggested. "It's kicking its mate in the belly....

Also put the dead man out of the roadway. 'E'll get mixed with the wheels."

Someone procured a rifle, placed the muzzle close to the animal's ear, and fired. The mule stretched its hind legs lazily out and ceased its struggles. Movement was resumed ahead, and dodging round the dead man, we continued our journey through the mud. It was difficult to make headway, our legs were knee-deep in slush, and the monstrous futility of shoving our way through, wearied us beyond telling. Only at rare intervals could we lift our feet clear of the ground and walk in comparative ease for a few moments. Now and again a machine gun opened on the moving throng, and bullets hummed by perilously close to our ears. The stretcher was a dead weight on us, and the poles cut into our shoulders.

The Scottish had charged across the road in the morning, and hundreds had come to grief. They were lying everywhere, out on the fields, by the roadside, and in the roadway mixed up with the mud. The driver who had been killed a moment ago was so preoccupied with his task that he had no time for any other work but his own. We were all like him. We had one job to do and that job took up our whole attention until it was completed. That was why our party did not put down our stretcher on the road and raise the dead from the mud; we walked over them.

How cold they looked, the kilted lads lying on their backs in the open, their legs, bare from knee to hip, white and ghostly in the wan light of the blazing ammunition depot at Lens.

Mud on the roadway, reaching to the axles of the limber wheels, dead men on the roadside, horses and mules tugging and straining at the creaking vehicles, wounded men on the stretchers; that was the picture of the night, and on we trudged, moving atoms of a pattern that kept continually repeating itself.

The mutilated and maimed who still lay out in the open called plaintively for succour. "For God's sake bring me away from here," a voice called. "I've been lying out this last four days." The man who spoke had been out since dawn, but periods of unconsciousness had disordered his count of time, and every conscious moment was an eternity of suffering.

We arrived at Q instead of Maroc, having missed the right turning. The village was crowded with men; a perfect village it was, with every house standing, though the civilian population had long since gone to other places. Two shells, monstrous twelve-inch terrors, that failed to explode, lay on the pavement at the entrance. We went past these gingerly, as ladies in dainty clothing might pass a fouling post, and carried our burden down the streets to the dressingstation. Outside the door were dozens of stretchers, and on each a stricken soldier, quiet and resigned, who gazed into the cheerless and unconcerned sky as if trying to find some deadened hope.

A Scottish regiment relieved from the trenches stood round a steaming dixie of tea, each man with a mess-tin in his hand. I approached the Jocks.

"Any tea to spare?" I asked one.

"Aye, mon, of course there's a drappie goin'," he answered, and handed me the mess-tin from which he had been drinking.

"How did you fare to-day?" I asked.

"There's a wheen o' us left yet," he replied with a solemn smile. "A dozen dixies of tea would nae gang far among us yesterday; but wi' one dixie the noo, we've some to spare.... Wha' d'ye belong tae?" he asked.

"The London Irish," I told him.

"'Twas your fellows that kicked the futba' across the field?"

"Yes."

"Into the German trench?"

"Not so far," I told the man. "A bullet hit the ball by the barbed-wire entanglements; I saw it lying there during the day."

"'Twas the maddest thing I've ever heard o'," said the Jock. "Hae ye lost many men?"

"A good number," I replied.

"I suppose ye did," said the man, but by his voice, I knew that he was not in-the least interested in our losses; not even in the issue of battle. In fact, few of us knew of the importance of the events in which we took part, and cared as little. If I asked one of our boys at that moment what were his thoughts he would answer, if he spoke truly: "I wonder when we're going to get relieved," or "I hope we're going to get a month's rest when we get out." Soldiers always speak of "we"; the individual is submerged in his regiment. We, soldiers, are part of the Army, the British Army, which will be remembered in days to come, not by a figurehead, as the fighters of Waterloo are remembered by Wellington, but as an army mighty in deed, prowess and endurance; an army which outshone its figureheads.

I went back to the dressing-station. Our wounded man was inside, and a young doctor was busy putting on a fresh dressing. The soldier was narrating the story of his wound.

"I was speaking to a stretcher-bearer about the ammunition depot afire in Lens," he was saying. "'Our shells hit it, and their bloomin' bullets 'ave copped me now,' I said, when something went siss! through my leg."

The man gazed round at the door and saw me.

"Wasn't that what I said, Pat?" he asked. "Yes," I answered. "You said that their *blooming* bullets had copped you." CHAPTER XI LOOS

The dead men lay on the cellar stair,
Toll of the bomb that found them there;
In the streets men fell as a bullock drops,
Sniped from the fringe of Hulluch copse.
And stiff in khaki the boys were laid—
Food of the bullet and hand-grenade—
This we saw when the charge was done,
And the East grew pale to the rising sun
In the town of Loos in the morning.

RIM of grey clouds clustered thick on the horizon as if hiding some wonderful secret from the eyes of men. Above my head the stars were twinkling, a soft breeze swung over the open, and moist gusts caught me in the face as I picked my way carefully through the still figures in brown and grey that lay all over the stony face of the level lands. A spinney on the right was wrapped in shadow, and when, for. a moment, I stood to listen, vague whispers and secret rustlings could be heard all around. The hour before the dawn was full of wonder, the world in which I moved was pregnant with mystery. "Who are these?" I asked myself as I looked at the still figures in khaki. "Where is the life, the vitality of yesterday's dawn; the fire of eager eyes, the mad pulsing of roving blood, and the great heart of young adventure? Has the roving, the vitality and the fire come to this; gone out like sparks from a star-shell falling in a pond? What are these things here? What am I? What is the purpose served by all this demolition and waste?" Like a child in the dark I put myself the question, but there was no answer. The stars wheel on their courses over the dance of death and the feast of joy, ever the same.

I walked up to the church by the trench through the graveyard where the white bones stuck out through the parapet. A pale mist gathered round the broken headstones and crept along the bushes of the fence. The Twin Towers stood in air—moody, apathetic, regardless of the shrapnel incense that the guns wafted against the lean girders. Sparrows twittered in the field, and a crow broke clumsily away from the branches in the spinney. A limber jolted along the road near me creaking and rumbling. On! driver, on! Get to Les Brebis before the dawn, and luck be with you! If the enemy sees you! On! on! I knew that he hurried; that one eye was on the east where the sky was flushing a faint crimson, and the other on the road in front where the dead mules grew more distinct and where the faces of trie dead men showed more clearly.

At that moment the enemy began to shell the road and the trench running parallel to it. I slipped into the shelter and waited. The transport came nearer, rolling and rumbling; the shrapnel burst violently. I cowered close to the parapet and I had a vivid mental picture of the driver leaning forward on the neck of his mule, his teeth set, his breath coming in short, sudden gasps. "Christ! am I going to get out of it?" he must have said. "Will dawn find me at Les Brebis?"

Something shot clumsily through the air and went plop! against the parados.

"Heavens! it's all up with me!" I said, and waited for the explosion. But there was none. I looked round and saw a leg on the floor of the trench, the leg of the transport driver, with its leg-iron shining like silver. The man's boot was almost worn through in the sole, and the upper was gashed as if with a knife. I'm sure it must have let in the wet.... And the man was alive a moment ago! The mule was still clattering along, I could hear the rumble of the wagon.... The firing ceased, and I went out in the open again.

I walked on the rim of the parapet and gazed into the dark streak of trench where the shadows clustered round traverse and dug-out door. In one bay a brazier was burning, and a bent figure of a man leant over a mess-tin of bubbling tea. All at once he straightened himself and looked up at me.

"Pat MacGill?" he queried.

"A good guess," I answered. "You're making breakfast early."

"A drop of tea on a cold morning goes down well," he answered. "Will you have a drop? I've milk and a sultana cake."

"How did you come by that?" I asked.

"In a dead man's pack," he told me, as he emptied part of the contents of the tin into a tin mug and handed it up.

The tea was excellent. A breeze swept over the parapet and ushered in the dawn. My heart fluttered like a bird; it was so happy, so wonderful to be alive, drinking tea from a sooty messtin on the parapet of the trench held by the enemy yesterday.

"It's quiet at present," I said.

"It'll soon not be quiet," said the man in the trench, busy now with a rasher of bacon which he was frying on his mess-tin lid. "Where have you come from?"

"I've been all over the place," I said. "Maroc, and along that way. You should see the road to Maroc. Muck to the knees; limbers, carts, wagons, guns, stretchers, and God knows what! going up and down. Dead and dying mules; bare-legged Jocks flat in the mud and wheels going across them. I'll never forget it."

"Nobody that has been through this will ever forget it," said the man in the trench. "I've seen more sights than enough. But nothing disturbs me now. I remember a year ago if I saw a man getting knocked down I'd run a mile; I never saw a dead person till I came here. Will you have a bit of bacon and fried bread?"

"Thanks," I answered, reaching down for the food. "It's very good of you."

"Don't mention it, Pat," he said, blushing as if ashamed of his kindness. "Maybe, it'll be my turn to come to you next time I'm hungry. Any word of when we're getting relieved?"

"I don't hear anything," I said. "Shortly, I hope. Many of your mates killed?" I asked.

"Many of them indeed," he replied. "Old L. went west the moment he crossed the top. He had only one kick at the ball. A bullet caught him in the belly. I heard him say 'A foul; a blurry foul!' as he went all in a heap. He was a sticker! Did you see him out there?"

He pointed a thumb to the field in rear.

"There are so many," I replied. "I did not come across him."

"And then B., D., and R., went," said the man in the trench. "B. with a petrol bomb, D. with shrapnel, and R. with a bayonet wound. Some of the Bavarians made a damned good fight for it."...

Round the traverse a voice rose in song, a trembling, resonant voice, and we guessed that sleep was still heavy in the eyes of the singer:

"There's a silver lining through the dark clouds shining, We'll turn the dark cloud inside out till the boys come home."

"Ah! it will be a glad day and a sorrowful day when the boys come home," said the man in the trench, handing me a piece of sultana cake. "The children will be cheering, the men will be cheering, the women—some of them. One woman will say: 'There's my boy, doesn't he look well in uniform?' Then another will say: 'Two boys I had, *they're* not here '"

I saw a tear glisten on the cheek of the boy below me, and something seemed to have caught in his throat. His mood craved privacy, I could tell that by the dumb appeal in his eyes.

"Good luck, matey," I mumbled, and walked away. The singer looked up as I was passing.

"Mornin', Pat," he said. "How goes it?"

"Not at all bad," I answered.

"Have you seen W.?" asked the singer.

"I've been talking to him for the last twenty minutes," I said. "He has given me half his breakfast.",

"I suppose he couldn't sleep last night," said the singer, cutting splinters of wood for the morning fire. "You've heard that his brother was killed yesterday morning?"

"Oh!" I muttered. "No, I heard nothing about it until now."

The dawn glowed crimson, streaks of red shot through the clouds to eastwards and touched the bowl of sky overhead with fingers of flame. From the dug-outs came the sound of sleepy voices, and a soldier out in open trench was cleaning his bayonet. A thin white fog lay close to the ground, and through it I could see the dead boys in khaki clinging, as it were, to the earth. I could see a long way round. Behind was the village where the wounded were dressed; how blurred it looked with its shell-scarred chimneys in air like the fingers of a wounded hand held up to a doctor. The chimneys, dun-tinted and lonely, stood silent above the mist, and here and there a tree which seemed to have been ejected from the brotherhood of its kind stood out in the open all alone. The smoke of many fires curled over the line of trenches. Behind the parapets lay many dead; they had fallen in the trench and their comrades had flung them out into the open. It was sad to see them there; yesterday or the day before their supple legs were strong for a long march; to-day

A shell burst dangerously near, and I went into the trench; the Germans were fumbling for their objective. Our artillery, as yet quiet, was making preparations for an anticipated German counter-attack, and back from our trench to Les Brebis, every spinney concealed a battery, every tree a gun, and every broken wall an ammunition depot. The dawning sun showed the terror of war quiet in gay disguise; the blue-grey, longnosed guns hidden in orchards where the apples lingered late, the howitzers under golden-fringed leaves, the metallic glint on the weapons' muzzles; the gunners asleep in adjacent dug-outs, their blankets tied tightly around their bodies, their heads resting on heavy shells, fit pillows for the men whose work dealt in death and destruction. The sleepers husbanded their energy for trying labour, the shells seemed to be saving their fury for more sure destruction. All our men were looking forward to a heavy day's work.

I went back to the dressing-station in Loos. The street outside, pitted with shell-holes, showed a sullen face to the leaden sky. The dead lay in the gutters, on the pavement, at the door-steps; the quick in the trenches were now consolidating our position, strengthening the trench which we had taken from the Germans. Two soldiers on guard stood at the door of the dressing-station. I dressed a few wounds and lit a cigarette.

"What's up with that fool?" said a voice at the door, and I turned to the man who spoke.

"Who?" I inquired.

"Come and see," said the man at the door. I looked up the street and saw one of our boys standing in the roadway and the smoke of a concussion shell coiling round his body. It was Bill Teake. He looked round, noticed us, and I could see a smile flower broadly on his face. He made a step towards us, halted and said something that sounded like "Yook! yook!" Then he took another step forward and shot out his hand as if playing bowls.

"He's going mad?" I muttered. "Bill, what are you doing?" I cried to him.

"Yook! yook! yook!" he answered in a coaxing voice.

"A bullet will give you yook! yook! directly," I cried. "Get under cover and don't be a fool." "Yook! yook!"

Then a shell took a neighbouring chimney away and a truckful of bricks assorted itself on the roadway in Bill's neighbourhood. Out of the smother of dust and lime a fowl, a long-necked black hen, fluttered into the air and flew towards our shelter. On the road in front it alighted and wobbled its head from one side to another in a cursory inspection of its position. Bill Teake came racing down the road.

"Don't frighten it away!" he yelled. "Don't shout. I want that 'en. It's my own 'en. I discovered it. Yook! yook! yook!"

He sobered his pace and approached the hen with cautious steps. The fowl was now standing on one leg, the other leg drawn up under its wing, its head in listening position, and its attitude betokened extreme dejection. It looked for all the world like Bill when he peers down the neck of a rum jar and finds the jar empty.

"Not a word now," said Teake, fixing one eye on me and another on the hen. "I must get my feelers on this 'ere cackler. It was up there sittin' atop of a dead Jock when I sees it.... Yook! yook! That's wot you must say to a bloomin' 'en w'en yer wants ter nab it.... Yook! yook! yook!"

He threw a crumb to the fowl. The hen picked it up, swallowed it, and hopped off for a little distance. Then it drew one leg up under its wing and assumed a look of philosophic calm.

"Clever hen!" I said.

"Damned ungrateful fraud!" said Bill angrily. "I've given it 'arf my iron rations. If it wasn't that I might miss it I'd fling a bully-beef tin at it."

"Where's your rifle?" I inquired.

"Left it in the trench," Bill replied. "I just came out to look for sooveneers. This is the only sooveneer I seen. Yook! yook! I'll sooveneer yer, yer swine. Don't yer understand yer own language?"

The hen made a noise like a chuckling frog.

"Yes, yer may uck! uck!" cried Bill, apostrophising the fowl. "I'll soon stop yer uck! uck! yer one-legged von Kluck! Where's a rifle to spare?"

I handed him a spare rifle which belonged to a man who had been shot outside the door that morning.

"Loaded?" asked Bill.

"Loaded," I lied.

The Cockney lay down on the roadway, stretched the rifle out in front, took steady aim, and pulled the trigger. A slight click was the only response.

"That's a dirty trick," he growled, as we roared with laughter. "A bloomin' Alleymong wouldn't do a thing like that."

So saying he pulled the bolt back, jerked a cartridge from the magazine, shoved a round into the breech and fired. The fowl fluttered in agony for a moment, then fell in a heap on the roadway. Bill handed the rifle back to me.

"I'll cook that 'en to-night," he said, with studied slowness. "It'll make a fine feed. 'En well cooked can't be beaten, and I'm damned if you'll get one bone to pick!"

"Bill!" I protested.

"Givin' me a hipe as wasn't loaded and sayin' it was," he muttered sullenly.

"I haven't eaten a morsel of hen since you pinched one at Mazingarbe," I said. "You remember that. 'Twas a damned smart piece of work."

A glow of pride suffused his face.

"Well, if there's any to spare to-night I'll let you know," said my mate. "Now I'm off."

"There's a machine gun playing on the road," I called to him, as he strolled off towards the trench with the hen under his arm. "You'd better double along."

He broke into a run, but suddenly stopped right in the centre of the danger zone. I could hear the bullets rapping on the cobblestones.

"I'll tell yer when the feed's ready, Pat," he called back. "You can 'ave 'arf the 'en for supper."

Then he slid off and disappeared over the rim of the trench.

CHAPTER XII RETREAT

"There's a battery snug in the spinney,
A French 'seventy-five' in the mine,
A big 'nine-point-two' in the village,
Three miles to the rear of the line.
The gunners will clean them at dawning,
And slumber beside them all day,
But the guns chant a chorus at sunset,
And then you should hear what they say." HE hour was one o'clock in the after noon, and a slight rain was now falling.

A dug-out in the bay leant wearily forward on its props; the floor of the trench, foul with blood and accumulated dirt, showed a weary face to the sky. A breeze had sprung up, and the watcher who looked over the parapet was met in the face with a soft, wet gust laden with rain swept off the grassy spot in front.... A gaunt willow peeped over the sandbags and looked timofous'v down at us. All the sandbags were perforated by machine-gun fire, a new gun was hidden on the rise on our right, but none of our observers could locate its position. On the evening before it had accounted for eighty-seven casualties; from the door of a house in Loos I had seen our men, who had attempted to cross the street, wiped out like flies. Very heavy fighting had been going on in the front line to the east of Hill 70 all through the morning. Several bomb attacks were made by the enemy, and all were repulsed. For the men in the front line trench the time was very trying. They had been subject to continual bomb attacks since the morning before.

"'Ow long 'ave we been 'ere?" asked Bill Teake, as he removed a clot of dirt from the foresight guard of his rifle. "I've lost all count of time."

"Not such a length of time," I told him.

"Time's long a-passin' 'ere," said Bill, leaning his head against the muddy parados. "Gawd, I'd like to be back in Les Brebis drinkin' beer, or 'avin' a bit of a kip for a change. When I go back to blighty I'll go to bed and I'll not get up for umpty-eleven months."

"We may get relieved to-morrow night," I said.

"To-morrow'll be another day nearer the day we get relieved, any'ow," said Bill sarcastically. "And another day nearer the end of the war," he added.

"I'm sick of it," he muttered, after a short silence. "I wish the damned war was blurry well finished. It gives me the pip. Curse the war! Curse everyone and everything! If the Alleymongs would come over now, I'd not lift my blurry 'ipe. I'd surrender; that's wot I'd do. Curse... Damn... Blast..."

I slipped to the wet floor of the trench asleep and lay there, only to awaken ten minutes later. I awoke with a start; somebody jumping over the parapet had planted his feet on my stomach. I rose from the soft earth and looked round. A kilted soldier was standing in the trench, an awkward smile on his face and one of his knees bleeding. Bill, who was awake, was gazing at the kiltie with wide open eyes.

The machine gun was speaking from the enemy's line, a shrewish tang in its voice, and little spurts of dirt flicked from our sandbags shot into the trench.

Bill's eyes looked so large that they surprised me; I had never seen him look in such a way before. What was happening? Several soldiers belonging to strange regiments were in our trench now; they were jumping over the parapet in from the open. One man I noticed was a nigger in khaki....

"They're all from the front trench," said Bill in a whisper of mysterious significance, and a disagreeable sensation stirred in my being.

"That means," I said, and paused.

"It means that the Allemongs are gettin' the best of it," said Bill, displaying an unusual interest in the action of his rifle. "They say the 2 ist and 24th Division are retreating from '111 70. Too 'ot up there. It's goin' to be a blurry row 'ere," he muttered. "But we're goin' to stick 'ere, wotever 'appens. No damned runnin' away with us!"

The trench was now crowded with strangers, and others were coming in. The field in front of our line was covered with figures running towards us. Some crouched as they ran, some tottered and fell; three or four crawled on their bellies, and many dropped down and lay where they fell.

The machine gun swept the field, and a vicious hail of shrapnel swept impartially over the quick, the wounded and the dead. A man raced up to the parapet which curved the bay in which I stood, a look of terror on his face. There he stood a moment, a timorous foot on a sandbag, calculating the distance of the jump... He dropped in, a bullet wound showing on the back of his tunic, and lay prostrate, face upwards on the floor of the trench. A second man jumped in on the face of the stricken man.

I hastened to help, but the newcomers pressed forward and pushed me along the trench. No heed was taken of the wounded man.

"Back! get back!" yelled a chorus of voices. "We've got to retire."

"'Oo the blurry 'ell said that?" I heard Bill Teake thunder. "If ye're not goin' to fight, get out of this 'ere place and die in the fields. Runnin' away, yer blasted cowards!"

No one seemed to heed him. The cry of "Back! back!" redoubled in violence. "We've got orders to retire! We must get back at once!" was the shout. "Make way there, let us get by."

It was almost impossible to stem the tide which swept up the trench towards Loos Road where the road leaves the village. I had a fleeting glimpse of one of our men rising on the fire position and gazing over the parapet. Even as he looked a bullet hit him in the face, and he dropped back, clawing at the air with his fingers.... Men still crowded in from the front, jumping on the struggling crush in the trench.... In front of me was a stranger, and in front of him was Rifleman Pryor, trying to press back against the oncoming men. A bullet ricochetted off a sandbag and hit the stranger on the shoulder and he fell face downwards to the floor. I bent to lift the wounded fellow and got pushed on top of him.

"Can you help him?" Pryor asked.

"If you can keep the crowd back," I muttered, getting to my feet and endeavouring to raise the fallen man.

Pryor pulled a revolver from his pocket, levelled it at the man behind me and shouted:

"If you come another step further I'll put a bullet through your head."

This sobered the soldier at the rear, who steadied himself by placing his hand against the traverse. Then he called to those who followed, "Get back! there's a wounded man on the floor of the trench."

A momentary halt ensued. Pryor and I gripped the wounded man, raised him on the parapet and pushed him into a shell-hole behind the sandbags. Lying flat on the ground up there I dressed the man's wounds. Pryor sat beside me, fully exposed to the enemy's fire, his revolver in his hand.

"Down, Pryor," I said several times. "You'll get hit."

"Oh, my time hasn't come yet," he said. "I'll not be done in this time, anyway. Fighting is going on in the front trench yet, and dozens of men are racing this way. Many of them are falling. I think some of our boys are firing at them, mistaking them for Germans.... Here's our colonel coming along the trench."

The colonel was in the trench when I got back there, exhorting his men to stand and make a fight of it. "Keep your backs to the walls, boys," he said, "and fight to the last."

The Irish had their back to the wall, no man deserted his post. The regiment at the moment was the backbone of the Loos front; if the boys wavered and broke the thousands of lives that were given to make a victory of Loos would have been lost in vain. Intrepid little Bill Teake, who was going to surrender to the first German whom he met, stood on the banquette, his jaw thrust forward determinedly and the light of battle in his eyes. Now and again he turned round and apostrophised the soldiers who had fallen back from the front line.

"Runnin' away!" he yelled. "Ugh.l Get back again and make a fight of it Go for the Allemongs just like you's go for rum rations."

The machine gun on the hill peppered Loos Road and dozens dropped there. The trench crossing the road was not more than a few feet deep at any time, and a wagon which had fallen in when crossing a hastily-constructed bridge the night before, now blocked the way. To pass across the men had to get up on the road, and here the machine gun found them; and all round the wagon bleeding bodies were lying three deep.

A young officer of the Regiment, whose men were carried away in the stampede, stood on the road with a Webley revolver in his hand and tried to urge his followers back to the front trench. "It's all a mistake," he shouted. "The Germans did not advance. The order to retire was a false one. Back again; boys, get back. Now, get back for the regiment's sake. If you don't we'll be branded with shame. Come now, make a stand and I'll lead you back again."

Almost simultaneously a dozen bullets hit him and he fell, his revolver still in his hand. Bill Teake procured the revolver at dusk....

Our guns came suddenly into play and a hellriot of artillery broke forth. Guns of all calibres were brought into work, and all spoke earnestly, madly, the 4 2's in the emplacement immediately to rear, the *g-2's* back at Maroc, and our big giants, the caterpillar howitzers, away behind further still. Gigantic shells swung over our heads, laughing, moaning, whistling, hooting, yelling. We could see them passing high up in air, looking for all the world like beer bottles flung from a juggler's hand. The messengers of death came from everywhere and seemed to be everywhere.

The spinney on the spur was churned, shivered, blown to pieces. Trees' uprooted rose twenty yards in the air, paused for a moment to take a look round, as it were, when at the zenith of their flight, then sank slowly/lazily to earth as if selecting a spot to rest upon. Two redbrick cottages with terracotta tiles which snuggled amidst the trees were struck simultaneously, and they went up in little pieces, save where one rafter rose hurriedly over the smoke and swayed, a clearly denned black line, in mid-air. Coming down abruptly it found a resting place on the branches of the trees. One of the cottages held a German gun and gunners.... Smoke, dust, lyddite fumes robed the autumn-tinted trees on the crest, the concussion shells burst into lurid flame, the shrapnel shells puffed high in air, and their white, ghostly smoke paled into the overcast heavens.

The retreat was stopped for a moment. The

Regiment recovered its nerve and fifty or sixty men rushed back. Our boys cheered.... But the renewed vitality was short-lived. A hail of shrapnel caught the party in the field and many of them fell. The nigger whom I had noticed earlier came running back, his teeth chattering, and flung himself into the trench. He lay on the floor and refused to move until Bill Teake gave him a playful prod with a bayonet. Our guns now spoke boisterously, and the German trenches on the hill were being blown to little pieces. Dug-outs were rioting, piecemeal, in air, parapets were crumbling hurriedly in and burying the men in the trench, bombs spun lazily in air, and the big caterpillar howitzers flung their projectiles across with a loud whoop of tumult. Our thousand and one guns were bellowing their terrible anthem of hate.

Pryor stood on the fire-step, his bayonet in one hand, an open tin of bully-beef in the other.

"There's no damned attack on at all," he said.

"A fresh English regiment came up and the got orders to retire for a few hundred yards to make way for them. Then there was some confusion, a telephone wire got broken, the retirement became a retreat. A strategic retreat, of course," said Pryor sarcastically, and pointed at the broken wagon on the Loos Road. "A strategic retreat," he muttered, and munched a piece of beef which he lifted from the tin with his fingers.

The spinney on which we had gazed so often now retained its unity no longer, the brick houses were gone; the lyddite clouds took on strange forms amidst the greenery, glided towards one another in a graceful waltz, bowed, touched tips, retired and paled away weary as it seemed of their fantastic dance. Other smoke bands of ashen hue intermixed with ragged, bilious-yellow fragments of cloud rose in the air and disappeared in the leaden atmosphere. Little wisps of vapour like feathers of some gigantic bird detached themselves from the horrible, diffused glare of bursting explosives, floated towards our parapet, and the fumes of poisonous gases caused us to gasp for breath. The shapelessness of Destruction reigned on the hill, a fitting accompaniment to the background of cloudy sky, dull, dark and wan.

Strange contrasts were evoked on the crest, monstrous heads rose over the spinney, elephants bearing ships, Vikings, bearded and savage, beings grotesque and gigantic took shape in the smoke and lyddite fumes.

The terrible assault continued without truce, interruption or respite; our guns scattered broadcast with prodigal indifference their apparently inexhaustible resources of murder and terror. The essence of the bombardment was in the furious succession of its blows. In the clamour and tumult was the crash and uproar of a vast bubbling cauldron forged and heated by the gods in ungodly fury.

The enemy would reply presently. Through the uproar I could hear the premonitory whispering of his guns regulating their range and feeling for an objective. A concussion shell whistled across the traverse in which I stood and in futile rage dashed itself to pieces on the level field behind. Another followed, crying like a child in pain, and finished its short, drunken career by burrowing into the red clay of the parados where it failed to explode. It passed close to my head, and fear went down into the innermost parts of me and held me for a moment.... A dozen shells passed over in the next few moments, rushing ahead as if they were pursued by something terrible, and burst in the open a hundred yards away. Then a livid flash lit a near dug-out; lumps of earth, a dozen beams and several sandbags changed their locality, and a man was killed by concussion. When the body was examined no trace of a wound could be seen. Up the street of Loos was a clatter and tumult. A house was flung to earth, making a noise like a statue falling downstairs in a giant's castle; iron girders at the coal-mine were wrenched and tortured, and the churchyard that bordered our trench had the remnants of its headstones flung about and its oft muddled graves dug anew by the shells.

The temporary bridge across the trench where it intersected the road, made the night before to allow ammunition limbers to pass, was blown sky high, and two men who sheltered under it were killed. Earth, splinters of wood and bits of masonry were flung into the trench, and it was wise on our part to lie on the floor or press close to the parapet. One man, who was chattering a little, tried to sing, but became silent when a comrade advised him "to hold his row; if the Germans heard the noise they might begin shelling."

The gods were thundering. At times the sound dwarfed me into such infinitesimal littleness that a feeling of security was engendered. In the midst of such an uproar and tumult, I thought that the gods, bent though they were upon destruction, would leave such a little atom as myself untouched. This for a while would give me a self-satisfied confidence in my own invulnerability.

At other times my being swelled to the grand chorus. I was one with it, at home in thunder. I accommodated myself to the Olympian uproar and shared in a play that would have delighted Jove and Mars. I had got beyond that mean where the soul of a man swings like a pendulum from fear to indifference, and from indifference to fear. In danger I am never indifferent, but I find that I can readily adapt myself to the moods and tempers of my environment. But all men have some restraining influence to help them in hours of trial, some principle or some illusion. Duty, patriotism, vanity, and dreams come to the help of men in the trenches, all illusions probably, ephemeral and fleeting; but for a man who is as ephemeral and fleeting as his illusions are, he can lay his back against them and defy death and the terrors of the world. But let him for a moment stand naked and look at the staring reality of the terrors that engirt him and he becomes a raving lunatic.

The cannonade raged for three hours,

then ceased with the suddenness of a stone falling to earth, and the ordeal was over.

As the artillery quietened the men who had just come into our trench plucked up courage again and took their way back to the front line of trenches, keeping well under the cover of the houses in Loos. In twenty minutes' time we were left to ourselves, nothing remained of those who had come our way save their wounded and their dead; the former we dressed and carried into the dressing-station, the latter we buried when night fell.

The evening came, and the greyish light of the setting sun paled away in a western sky, leadenhued and dull. The dead men lying out in the open became indistinguishable in the gathering darkness. A deep silence settled over the village, the roadway and trench, and with the quiet came fear. I held my breath. What menace did the dark world contain? What threat did the ghostly star-shells, rising in air behind the Twin Towers, breathe of? Men, like ghosts, stood on the banquettes waiting, it seemed, for something to take place. There was no talking, no laughter. The braziers were still unlit, and the men had not eaten for many hours. But none set about to prepare a meal. It seemed as if all were afraid to move lest the least noise should awake the slumbering Furies. The gods were asleep and it was unwise to disturb them....

A limber clattered up the road and rations were dumped down at the corner of the village street.

"I 'ope they've brought the rum," somebody remarked, and we all laughed boisterously. The spell was broken, and already my mate, Bill Teake, had applied a match to a brazier and a little flame glowed at the corner of a traverse. Now was the moment to cook the hen which he had shot that morning.

As he bent over his work, someone coming along the trench stumbled against him, and nearly threw Bill into the fire.

"'Oo the blurry 'ell is that shovin' about," spluttered Teake, rubbing the smoke from his eyes and not looking round.

"It's the blurry Colonel of the London Irish," a voice replied, and Bill shot up to attention and saluted his commanding officer.

"I'm sorry, sir," he said.
"It's all right," said the officer. "If I was in your place, I might have said worse things."

Bill recounted the incident afterwards and concluded by saying, "'E's a fine bloke, 'e is, our CO. I'd do anythink for him now." CHAPTER XIII

A PRISONER OF WAR

A star-shell holds the sky beyond
Shell-shivered Loos, and drops
In million sparkles on a pond
That lies by Hulluch copse.
A moment's brightness in the sky, To vanish at a breath,
And die away, as soldiers die
Upon the wastes of death.

HERE'LL be some char (tea) in a minute," said Bill, as he slid over the parapet into the trench. "I've got some cake, a tin of sardines and a box of cigars, fat ones."

"You've been at a dead man's pack," I said.

"The dead don't need nuffink," said Bill.

It is a common practice with the troops after a charge to take food from the packs of their fallen comrades. Such actions are inevitable; when crossing the top, men carry very little, for too much weight is apt to hamper their movements.

Transports coming along new roads are liable to delay, and in many cases they get blown out of existence altogether. When rations arrive, if they arrive, they are not up to the usual standard, and men would go hungry if death did not come in and help them. As it happens, however, soldiers feed well after a charge.

Bill lit a candle in the German dug-out, applied a match to a brazier and placed his mess-tin on the flames. The dug-out with its flickering taper gave me an idea of cosiness, coming in as I did from the shell-scarred village and its bleak cobbled streets. To sit down here on a sandbag (Bill had used the wooden seats for a fire) where men had to accommodate themselves on a pigmy scale, was very comfortable and reassuring. The light of the candle and brazier cast a spell of subtle witchery on the black walls and the bayonets gleaming against the roof, but despite this, innumerable shadows lurked in the corners, holding some dark council.

"Ha!" said Bill, red in the face from his exertions over the fire. "There's the water singin' in the mess-tin; it'll soon be dancin'."

The water began to splutter merrily as he spoke, and he emptied the tea on the tin which he lifted from the brazier with his bayonet. From his pack he brought forth a loaf and cut it into good thick slices.

"Now some sardines, and we're as comfy as kings," he muttered. "We'll 'ave a meal fit for a gentleman, any gentleman in the land."

"What sort of meal is fit for a gentleman?" I asked.

"Oh! a real good proper feed," said Bill. "Suthin' that fills the guts."

The meal was fit for a gentleman indeed; in turn we drank the tea from the mess-tin and lifted the sardines from the tin with our fingers; we had lost our forks as well as most of our equipment.

"What are you goin' to do now?" asked Bill, when we had finished.

"I don't know that there's anything to be done in my job," I said. "All the wounded have been taken in from here."

"There's no water to be got," said Bill. "There's a pump in the street, but nobody knows whether it's poisoned or not. The nearest well that's safe to drink from is at Maroc."

"Is there a jar about?" I asked Bill, and he unearthed one from the corner of his jacket. "I'll go to Maroc and bring up a jar of water," I said. "I'll get back by midnight, if I'm not strafed."

I went out on the road. The night had cleared and was now breezy; the moon rode high amongst scurrying clouds, the trees in the fields were harassed by a tossing motion and leant towards the village as if seeking to get there. The grasses shivered, agitated and helpless, and behind the Twin Towers of Loos the star-shells burst into many-coloured flames and showed like a summer flower-garden against the sky. A windmill, with one wing intact, stood out, a ghostly phantom, on a rise overlooking Hulluch.

The road to Maroc was very quiet and almost deserted; the nightly traffic had not yet begun, and the nightly connonade was as yet merely fumbling for an opening. The wrecks of the previous days were still lying there; long-eared mules immobile in the shafts of shattered limbers, dead Highlanders with their white legs showing wan in the moonlight, boys in khaki with their faces pressed tightly against the cobblestones, broken wagons, discarded stretchers, and derelict mailbags with their rain-sodden parcels and letters from home.

Many wounded were still lying out in the fields. I could hear them calling for help and groaning.

"How long had they lain there?" I asked myself. "Two days, probably. Poor devils!"

I walked along, the water jar knocking against my legs. My heart was filled with gloom. "What is the meaning of all this?" I queried. "This wastage, this hell?"

A white face peered up at me from a ditch by the roadside, and a weak voice whispered, "Matey!"

"What is it, chummy?" I queried, coming close to the wounded man.

"Can you get me in?" he asked. "I've been out for—oh! I don't know how long," he moaned.

"Where are you wounded?" I asked.

"I got a dose of shrapnel, matey," he said. "One bullet caught me in the heel, another in the shoulder."

"Has anybody dressed the wounds?" I asked. "Aye, aye," he answered. "Somebody did, then went off and left me here."

"Do you think you could grip me tightly round the shoulders if I put you on my back?" I said. "I'll try and carry you in."

"We'll give it a trial," said the man in a glad voice, and I flung the jar aside and hoisted him on my back.

Already I was worn out with having had no sleep for two nights, and the man on my back was heavy. For awhile I tried to walk upright, but gradually my head came nearer the ground.

"I can't go any further," I said at last, coming to a bank on the roadside and resting my burden. "I feel played out. I'll see if I can get any help. There's a party of men working over there. I'll try and get a few to assist me.

The man lay back on the grass and did not answer. Probably he had lost consciousness.

A Scotch regiment was at work in the field, digging trenches; I approached an officer, a dark, low set man with a heavy black moustache.

"Could you give me some men to assist me to carry in wounded?" I asked. "On each side of the road there are dozens"

"Can't spare any men," said the officer. "Haven't enough for the work here. "

"Many of your own countrymen are out there," I said.

"Can't help it," said the man. "We all have plenty of work here."

I glanced at the man's shoulder and saw that he belonged to "The Lone Star Crush"; he was a second-lieutenant. Second-lieutenants fight well, but lack initiative.

A captain was directing work near at hand, and I went up to him.

"I'm a stretcher-bearer," I said. "The fields round here are crowded with wounded who have been lying out for ever so long. I should like to take them into the dressing-station. Could you give me some men to help me?"

"Do you come from the Highlands?" asked the captain.

"No, I come from Ireland," I said.

"Oh!" said the officer; then inquired: "How many men do you want?"

"As many as you can spare."

"Will twenty do?" I was asked.

I went down the road in charge of twenty men, stalwart Highlanders, massive of shoulder and thew, and set about collecting the wounded. Two doors, a barrow and a light cart were procured, and we helped the stricken men on these conveyances. Some men were taken away across the Highlanders' shoulders, and some who were not too badly hurt limped in with one man to help each case. The fellow whom I left lying by the roadside was placed on a door and borne away.

I approached another officer, a major this time, and twelve men were handed over to my care; again six men were found and finally eight who set about their work like Trojans.

My first twenty returned with wheeled and hand stretchers, and scoured the fields near Loos. By dawn fifty-three wounded soldiers were taken in by the men whom I got to assist me, and I made my way back to the trench with a jar full of water. Wild, vague, and fragmentary thoughts rioted through my mind, and I was conscious of a wonderful exhilaration. I was so pleased with myself that I could dance along the road and sing with pure joy. Whether the mood was brought about by my success in obtaining men or saving wounded I could not determine. Anyhow, I did not attempt to analyse the mood; I was happy and I was alive, with warm blood palpitating joyously through my veins.

I found a full pack lying in the road beside a dead mule which lay between the shafts of a limber. The animal's ears stuck perkily up like birds on a fence.

In the pack I found an overcoat, a dozen bars of chocolate, and a piece of sultana cake.

I crossed the field. The darkness hung heavy as yet, and it was difficult to pick one's way. Now I dropped into a shell-hole and fell flat on my face, and again my feet got entangled in lines of treacherous trip-wire, and I went headlong.

"Halt!"

I uttered an exclamation of surprise and fear, and stopped short a few inches from the point of a bayonet. Staring into the darkness I discerned the man who had ordered me to halt. One knee was on the ground, and a white hand clutched the rifle barrel. I could hear him breathing heavily.

"What's wrong with you, man?" I asked.

"'Oo are yer?" inquired the sentry.

"A London Irish stretcher-bearer," I said.

"Why are yer comin' through our lines?" asked the sentry.

"I'm just going back to the trench," I said. "I've been taking a wounded man down to Maroc."

"To where?" asked the man with the bayonet.

"Oh! it seems as if you don't know this place," I said. "Are you new to this part of the world?"

The man made no answer, he merely shoved his bayonet nearer my breast and whistled softly. As if in reply to this signal, two forms took shape in the darkness and approached the sentry.

"What's wrong?" asked one of the newcomers.

"This 'ere bloke comes up just now," said the sentry, pointing the bayonet at my face. "'E began to ask me questions and I 'ad my suspicions, so I whistled."

"That's right," said one of the newcomers, rubbing a thoughtful hand over the bayonet which he carried; then he turned to me. "Come along wiv us," he said, and, escorted by the two soldiers, I made my way across the field towards a ruined building which was raked at intervals by the German artillery. The field was peopled with soldiers lying flat on waterproof sheets, and many of the men were asleep. None had been there in the early part of the night.

An officer, an elderly man with a white moustache, sat under the shade of the building holding an electric lamp in one hand and writing in a notebook with the other. We came to a halt opposite him.

"What have you here?" he asked, looking at one of my captors.

"We found this man inquiring what regiment was here and if it had just come," said the soldier on my right who, by the stripes on his sleeve, I perceived was a corporal. "He aroused our suspicions and we took him prisoner."

"What is your name?" asked the officer, turning to me.

I told him. As I spoke a German shell whizzed over our heads and burst about three hundred yards to rear. The escort and the officer went flop to earth and lay there for the space of a second.

"You don't need to duck," I said. "That shell burst half a mile away."

"Is that so?" asked the officer, getting to his feet. "I thought it Oh! what's your name?"

I told him my name the second time.

"That's your real name?" he queried.

I assured him that it was, but my assurance was lost, for a second shell rioted overhead, and the escort and officer went again flop to the cold ground.

"That shell has gone further than the last," I said to the prostrate figures. "The Germans are shelling the road on the right; it's a pastime of theirs."

"Is that so?" asked the officer, getting to his feet again. Then, hurriedly, "What's your regiment?"

Before I had time to reply, three more prisoners were taken in under escort; I recognised Pryor as one of them. He carried a jar of water in his hand.

"Who are these?" asked the officer.

"They came up to the sentry and asked questions about the regiment," said the fresh escort. "The sentry's suspicions were aroused and he signalled to us, and we came forward and arrested these three persons."

The officer looked at the prisoners.

"What are your names, your regiments?" he asked. "Answer quickly. I've no time to waste."

"May I answer, sir?" I asked.

"What have you to say?" inquired the officer.

"Hundreds of men cross this field nightly," I said. "Working-parties, ration-fatigues, stretcher-bearers and innumerable others cross here. They're going up and down all night. By the way you duck when a shell passes high above you, I judge that you have just come out here. If you spend your time taking prisoners all who break through your line" (two fresh prisoners were brought in as I spoke) "you'll be busy asking English soldiers questions till dawn. I hope I don't offend you in telling you this."

The officer was deep in though, for a moment; then he said to me, "Thanks very much, you can return to your battalion." I walked away. As I went off I heard the officer speak to the escorts.

"You'd better release these men," he said. "I find this field is a sort of public thoroughfare."

A brigade was camped in the field, I discovered. The next regiment I encountered took me prisoner also; but a few shells dropped near at hand and took up the attention of my captor for a moment. This was an opportunity not to be missed; I simply walked away from bondage and sought the refuge of my own trench.

"Thank goodness," I said, as I slid over the parapet. "I'll have a few hours' sleep now."

But there was no rest for me. A few of our men, weary of the monotony of the dug-out, had crept up to the German trench, where they amused themselves by flinging bombs on the enemy. As if they had not had enough fighting!

On my return they were coming back in certain stages of demolition. One with a bullet in his foot, another with a shell-splinter in his cheek, and a third without a thumb.

These had to be dressed and taken into Maroc before dawn.

A stretcher-bearer at the front has little of the excitement of war, and weary hours of dull work come his way when the excitement is over.

CHAPTER XIV THE CHAPLAIN

The moon looks down upon a ghost-like figure, Delving a furrow in the cold, damp sod,

The grave is ready, and the lonely digger

Leaves the departed to their rest and God.

I shape a little cross and plant it deep

To mark the dug-out where my comrades sleep.

IWISH I was in the Ladies' Volunteer Corps," said Bill Teake next day, as he sat on the fire-step of the trench and looked at the illustrated daily which had been used in packing a parcel from home.

"Why?" I asked.

"They were in bathing last week," said Teake. "Their picture is here; fine girls they are, too! Oh, blimey I" Bill exclaimed as he glanced at the date on the paper. "This 'ere photo was took last June."

"And this is the 28th of September," said Pryor.

We needed a rest now, but we still were in the trenches by the village, holding on and hoping that fresh troops would come up and relieve us.

"Anything about the war in that paper, Bill?" someone asked.

"Nuthin' much," Bill answered. "The Bishop of says this is a 'oly war.... Blimey,

'e's talkin' through 'is 'at. 'Oly, indeed, it's 'oly 'ell. D'ye mind when 'e came out 'ere, this 'ere Bishop, an' told us 'e carried messages from our wives, our fathers an' mothers. If I was a married bloke I'd 'ave arst 'im wot did 'e mean by takin' messages from my old woman."

"You interpreted the good man's remarks literally," said Pryor, lighting a cigarette. "That was wrong. His remarks were bristling with metaphors. He spoke as a man of God so that none could understand him. He said, as far as I can remember, that we could face death without fear if we were forgiven men; that it was wise to get straight with God, and the blood of Christ would wash our sins away, and all the rest of it."

"Stow it, yer bloomin' fool," said Bill Teake. "Yer don't know what yer jawin' about. S'pose a bishop 'as got ter make a livin' like ev'ryone else; an' 'e's got ter work for it. 'Ere's somethin' about parsons in this paper. One is askin' if a man in 'oly Orders should take up arms or not."

"Of course not," said Pryor. "If the parsons take up arms, who'll comfort the women at home when we're gone?"

"The slackers will comfort them," some one remarked. "I've a great respect for slackers. They'll marry our sweethearts when we're dead."

"We hear nothing of a curates' regiment," I said. "In a Holy War young curates should lead the way."

"They'd make damned good bomb throwers," said Bill.

"Would they swear when making a charge?" I inquired.

"They wouldn't beat us at that," said Bill.

"The holy line would go praying down to die,' parodied Pryor, and added: "A chaplain may be a good fellow, you know."

"It's,a woman's job," said Bill Teake. "Blimey! s'pose women did come out 'ere to comfort us, I wouldn't 'arf go mad with joy. I'd give my last fag, I'd give—oh! anything to see the face of an English girl now.... They say in the papers that hactresses come out 'ere. We've never seen one, 'ave we?"

"Actresses never come out here," said Pryor. "They give a performance miles back to the R.A.M.C., Army Service Corps, and Mechanical Transport men, but for us poor devils in the trenches there is nothing at all, not even decent pay."

"Wot's the reason that the more danger men go into the less their pay?" asked Teake. "The further a man's back from the trenches the more 'e gets."

"Mechanical Transport drivers have a trade that takes a long apprenticeship," said Pryor. "Years perhaps"

"'Aven't we a trade, too?" asked Bill. "A damned dangerous trade, the most dangerous in the world?"

"What's this?" I asked, peeping over the parados to the road in our rear. "My God! there's a transport wagon going along the road!"

"Blimey! you're sprucing," said Bill, peeping over; thenlhis eye fell on a wagon drawn by two mules going along the highway. "Oh, the damned fools, goin' up that way. They'll not get far."

The enemy occupied a rise on our right, and a machine gun hidden somewhere near the trench swept that road all night. The gun was quiet all day long; no one ventured along there before dusk. A driver sat in front of the wagon, leaning back a little, a whip in his hand. Beside him sat another soldier.... Both were going to their death, the road at a little distance ahead crossed the enemy's trench.

"They have come the wrong way," I said. "They were going to Loos, I suppose, and took the wrong turning at the Valle Crossroads. Poor devils!"

A machine gun barked from the rise; we saw the driver of the wagon straighten himself and look round. His companion pointed a finger at the enemy's trench....

"For Christ's sake get off!" Bill shouted at them; but they couldn't hear him, the wagon was more than a quarter of a mile away from our trench.

"Damn it!" exclaimed Bill; "they'll both be killed. There!"

The vehicle halted; the near-side wheeler shook its head, then dropped sideways on the road, and kicked out with its hind legs, the other animal fell on top of it. The driver's whip went flying from his hands, and the man lurched forward and fell on top of the mules. For a moment he lay there, then with a hurried movement he slipped across to the other side of the far animal and disappeared. Our eyes sought the other soldier, but he was gone from sight, probably he had been shot off his seat.

"The damned fools!" I muttered. "What brought them up that way?"

"Wot's that?" Bill suddenly exclaimed. "See, comin' across the fields behind the road! A man, a hofficer.... Another damned fool, 'im; 'e'll get a bullet in 'im."

Bill pointed with his finger, and we looked. Across the fields behind that stretched from the road to the ruined village of Maroc we saw for the moment a man running towards the wagon. We only had a momentary glimpse then. The runner suddenly fell flat into a shell-hole and disappeared from view.

"He's hit," said Pryor. "There, the beastly machine gun is going again. Who is he?"

We stared tensely at the shell-hole. No sign of movement....

"'E's done in," said Bill.

Even as he spoke the man who had fallen rose and raced forward for a distance of fifty yards and flung himself flat again. The machine gun barked viciously....

Then followed a tense moment, and again the officer (we now saw that he was an officer) rushed forward for several yards and precipitated himself into a shell-crater. He was drawing nearer the disabled wagon at every rush. The machine gun did not remain silent for a moment now; it spat incessantly at the fields.

"He's trying to reach the wagon," I said. "I don't envy him his job, but, my God, what pluck!"

"'Oo is 'e?" asked Bill. "'E's not arf a brick, 'ooever 'e is!"

"I think I know who it is," said Pryor. "It's the Roman Catholic chaplain, Father Lane-Fox. He's a splendid man. He came over with us in the charge, and he helped to carry out the wounded till every man was in. Last night when we went for our rations he was helping the sanitary squad to bury the dead; and the enemy were shelling all the time. He is the pluckiest man in Loos."

"He wanted to come across in the charge," I said, "but the Brigadier would not allow him. An hour after we crossed the top I saw him in the second German trench.... There he is, up again!"

The chaplain covered a hundred yards in the next spurt; then he flung himself to earth about fifty yards from the wagon. The next lap was the last; he reached the wagon and disappeared. We saw nothing more of him that day. At night when I went down to the dressing-station at Maroc I was told how the chaplain had brought a wounded transport driver down to the dressing-station after dusk. The driver had got three bullets through his arm, one in his shoulder, one in his foot, and two in the calf of his leg. The driver's mate had been killed; a bullet pierced his brain.

The London Irish love Father Lane-Fox; he visited the men in the trenches daily, and all felt the better for his coming.

Often at night the sentry on watch can see a dark form between the lines working with a shovel and spade burying the dead. The bullets whistle by, hissing of death and terror; now and then a bomb whirls in air and bursts loudly; a shell screeches like a bird of prey; the hounds of war rend the earth with frenzied fangs; but indifferent to all the clamour and tumult the solitary digger bends over his work burying the dead.

"It's old Father Lane-Fox," the sentry will mutter. "He'll be killed one of these fine days." CHAPTER XV

A LOVER AT LOOS

The turrets twain that stood in air
Sheltered a foeman sniper there;
They found who fell to the sniper's aim,
A field of death on the field of fame—
And stiff in khaki the boys were laid,
To the rifle's toll at the barricade;
But the quick went clattering through the town,
Shot at the sniper and brought him down,
In the town of Loos in the morning.

iHE night was wet, the rain dripped from the sandbags and lay in little pools on the floor of the trench. Snug in the shelter of its keep a machine gun lurked privily, waiting for blood. The weapon had an absolutely impersonal air; it had nothing to do with war and the maiming of men. Two men were asleep in the bay, sitting on the fire-step and snoring loudly. A third man leant over the parapet, his eyes (if they were open) fixed on the enemy's trench in front. Probably he was asleep; he stood fixed to his post motionless as a statue. I wrapped my overcoat tightly round my body and lay down in the slush by a dug-out door. The dug-out, a German construction that burrowed deep in the chalky clay of Loos, was crowded with queer, distorted figures. It looked as if the dead on the field had been collected and shovelled into the place pell-mell. Bill Teake lay with his feet inside the shelter, his head and shoulders out in the rain. "I couldn't get in nohow," he grumbled as I lay down; "so I arst them inside to throw me a 'andful of fleas an' I'd kip on the doorstep. Blimey! 'tain't arf a barney; mud feathers, and no blurry blanket. There's one thing certain, anyhow, that is, in the Army you're certain to receive what you get."

I was asleep immediately, my head on Bill's breast, my body in the mud, my clothes sodden with rain. In the nights that followed Loos we slept anywhere and anyhow. Men lay in the mud in the trenches, in the fields, by the roadside, on sentry, and out on listening patrols between the lines. I was asleep for about five minutes when someone woke me up. I got to my feet, shivering with cold.

"What's up?" I asked the soldier who had shaken me from my slumber. He was standing opposite, leaning against the parados and yawning.

"There's a bloke in the next dug-out as 'as got wounded," said the man "'E needs someone to dress 'is wound an' take 'im to the dressin'station. 'E 'as just crawled in from the fields."

"All right," I replied. "I'll go along and see him."

A stairway led down to the dug-out; an officer lay asleep at the entrance, and a lone cat lay curled up on the second step. At the bottom of the stair was a bundle of khaki, moaning feebly.

"Much hurt?" I asked.

"Feelin' a bit rotten," replied a smothered voice.

"Where's your wound?"
"On my left arm."

"What is your regiment?" I asked, fumbling at the man's sleeve.

"The East Yorks," was the reply to my question. "I was comin' up the trench that's piled with dead Germans. I couldn't crawl over them all the way, they smelt so bad. I got up and tried to walk; then a sniper got me."

"Where's your regiment?" I asked.

"I don't know," was the answer. "I got lost and I went lookin' for my mates. I came into a trench that was crowded with Germans."

"There's where you got hit," I said.

"No; they were Germans that wasn't dead," came the surprising reply. "They were cooking food."

"When was this?" I asked.

"Yesterday, just as it was growin' dusk," said the wounded man in a weary voice. "Then the Germans saw me and they began to shout and they caught hold of their rifles. I jumped over the trench and made off with bullets whizzin' all round me. I tripped and fell into a shell-hole and I lay there until it was very dark. Then I got into the English trenches. I 'ad a sleep till mornin', then I set off to look for my regiment."

While he was speaking I had lit the candle which I always carried in my pocket and placed it on the floor of the dug-out. I examined his wound. A bullet had gone through the left forearm, cutting the artery and fracturing the bone; the blood was running down to his finger tips in little rivulets. I looked at the face of the patient. He was a mere boy, with thoughtful dark eyes, a snub nose, high cheekbones; a line of down showed on a long upper lip, and a fringe of innocent curling hairs straggled down his cheeks and curved round his chin. He had never used a razor.

I bound up the wound, found a piece of bread in my pocket and gave it to him. He ate ravenously.

"Hungry?" I said.

"'As a 'awk," he answered. "I didn't 'ave nothin' to-day and not much yesterday."

"How long have you been out here?" I asked.

"Only a week," he said. "The regiment marched from to here. 'Twasn't 'arf a bloomin' sweat. We came up and got into action at once."

"You'll be going home with this wound," I said.

"Will I?" he asked eagerly.

"Yes," I replied. "A fracture of the forearm. It will keep you in England for six months. How do you like that?"

"I'll be pleased," he said.

"Have you a mother?" I asked.

"No, but I've a girl."

"Oh!"

"Not 'arf I 'aven't," said the youth. "I've only one, too. I don't 'old with foolin' about with women. One's enough to be gone on, and often one is one too many."

"Very sound reasoning," I remarked sleepily. I had sat down on the floor and was dozing off.

The officer at the top of the stair stirred, shook himself and glanced down.

"Put out that light," he growled. "It's showing out of the door. The Germans will see it and send a shell across."

I put the candle out and stuck it in my pocket.

"Are you in pain now?" I asked the wounded boy.

"There's no pain now," was the answer. "It went away when you put the dressing on."

"Then we'll get along to the dressing-station," I said, and we clambered up the stairs into the open trench.

The sky, which was covered with dark grey clouds when I came in, had cleared in parts, and from time to time the moon appeared like a soft beautiful eye. The breezes held converse on the sandbags. I could hear the subdued whispering of their prolonged consultation. We walked along the peopled alley of war, where the quick stood on the banquettes, their bayonets reflecting the brilliance of the moon. When we should get as far as the trench where the dead Germans were lying we would venture into the open and take the high road to Maroc.

"So you've got a girl," I said to my companion.

"I have," he answered. "And she's not 'arf a one either. She's a servant in a gentleman's

'ouse at Y-. I was workin' for a baker and

I used to drive the van. What d'ye work at?" i "I'm a navvy," I said. "I dig drains and things like that."

"Not much class that sort of work," said the baker's boy. "If you come to Y -after the war I'll try and get yer a job at the baker's.... Well, I saw this 'ere girl at the big 'ouse and I took a fancy to 'er. Are yer much gone on girls? No, neither am I gone on any, only this one. She's a sweet thing. I'd read you the last letter she sent me only it's too dark. Maybe I could read it if the moon comes out. Can you read a letter by the light of the moon? No. ... Well, I took a fancy to the girl and she fell in love with me. 'Er name was Polly Pundy. What's your name?" "Socrates," I said.

"My name is plain Brown," the boy said. "Jimmy Brown. My mates used to call me Tubby because I was stout. Have you got a nickname? No.... I don't like a nickname. Neither does Polly."

"How does your love affair progress?" I asked.

"It's not all 'oney," said the youth, trying to evade a projecting sandbag that wanted to nudge his wounded arm.

"It makes one think. Somehow, I like that 'ere girl too well to be 'appy with 'er. She's too good for me, she is. I used to be jealous sometimes; I would strike a man as would look at 'er as quick as I'd think of it. Sometimes when a young feller passed by and didn't look at my Polly I'd be angry too. 'Wasn't she good enough for 'im?' I'd say to myself; usin' 'is eyes to look at somethin' else when Polly is about"

"We'll get over the top now," I said, interrupting Brown. We had come to the trench of the dead Germans. In front of us lay a dark lump coiled up in the trench; a hand stretched out towards us, a wan face looked up at the grey sky.... "We'll speak of Polly Pundy out in the open."

We crossed the sandbagged parados. The level lay in front—grey, solitary, formless. It was very quiet, and in the silence of the fields where the whirlwind of war had spent its fury a few days ago there was a sense of eternal loneliness and sadness. The grey calm night toned the moods of my soul into one of voiceless sorrow, containing no element of unrest. My mood was well in keeping with my surroundings. In the distance I could see the broken chimney of Maroc coal-mine standing forlorn in the air. Behind, the Twin Towers of Loos quivered, grimly spectral.

"We'll walk slowly, Brown," I said to the wounded boy. "We'll fall over the dead if we're not careful.... Is Polly Pundy still in the gentleman's house?" I asked.

"She's still there," said the boy. "When we get married we're goin' to open a little shop."

"A baker's shop?" I asked.

"I s'pose so. It's what I know more about than anythink else. D'you know anything about baking.... Nothing? It's not a bad thing to turn your 'and to, take my tip for it.... Ugh! I almost fell over a dead bloke that time.... I'm sleepy, aren't you?"

"By God! I am sleepy, Jimmy Brown," I muttered. "I'll try and find a cellar in Maroc when I get there and have a good sleep."

The dressing-station in the ruined village was warm and comfortable. An R.A.M.C. orderly was busily engaged in making tea for the wounded who lay crowded in the cellar waiting until the motor ambulances came up. Some had waited for twenty-four hours. Two doctors were busy with the wounded, a German officer with an arm gone lay on a stretcher on the floor; a cat was asleep near the stove, I could hear it purring.

Mick Garney, one of our boys, was lying on the stretcher near the stove. He was wounded in the upper part of the thigh, and was recounting his adventures in the charge. He had a queer puckered little face, high cheekbones, and a little black clay pipe, which he always carried inside his cap on parade and in his haversack on the march, that was of course when he was not carrying it between his teeth with its bowl turned down. Going across in the charge, Micky observed some half a dozen Germans rushing out from a spinney near Hill 70, and placing a machine gun on the Vermelles-Hulluch road along which several kilted Highlanders were coming at the double. Garney took his pipe out of his mouth and looked on. They were daring fellows, those Germans, coming out into the open in the face of a charge and placing their gun in position. "I must stop their game," said Mick.

He lit his pipe, turned the bowl down, then lay on the damp earth and, using a dead German for a rifle-rest, he took careful aim. At the pull of the trigger, one of the Germans fell headlong, a second dropped and a third. The three who remained lugged the gun back into Loos churchyard and placed it behind a tombstone on which was the figure of two angels kneeling in front of "The Sacred Heart." Accompanied by two bombers, Mick Garney found the Germans there.

"God forgive me!" said Mick, recounting the incident to the M.O., "I threw a bomb that blew the two angels clean off the tombstone."

"And the Germans?" asked the M.O.

"Begorra! they went with the angels. " ... A doctor, a pot-bellied man with a kindly face and an innocent moustache, took off Brown's bandage and looked at me.

"How are things going on up there?" he asked.

"As well as might be expected," I replied. "You look worn out," said the doctor. "I feel worn out," I answered. "Is it a fact that the German Crown Prince has been captured?" asked the doctor. "Who?"

"The German Crown Prince," said the man. "A soldier who has just gone away from here vows that he saw Little Willie under escort in Loos."

"Oh, it's all bunkum," I replied. "I suppose the man has had too much rum. " The doctor laughed.

"Well, sit down and I'll see if I can get you a cup of tea," he said in a kindly voice, and at his word I sat down on the floor. I was conscious of nothing further until the following noon. I awoke to find myself in a cellar, wrapped in blankets and lying on a stretcher. I went upstairs and out into the street and found that I had been sleeping in the cellar of the house adjoining the dressing-station.

I called to mind Jimmy Brown, his story of Polly Pundy; his tale of passion told on the field of death, his wound and his luck. A week in France only, and now going back again to England, to Polly Pundy, servant in a gentleman's house. He was on his way home now probably, a wound in his arm and dreams of love in his head. You lucky devil, Jimmy Brown!... Anyhow, good fortune to you.... But meanwhile it was raining and I had to get back to the trenches.

CHAPTER XVI THE RATION PARTY

"In trie Army you are certain to receive what you get."— Trench Proverb. RIFLEMAN lay snoring in the soft slush on the floor of the trench, his arms doubled under him, his legs curved up so that the knees reached the man's jaw As I touched him he shuffled a little, turned on his side, seeking a more comfortable position in the mud, and fell asleep again. A light glowed in the dug-out and someone in there was singing in a low voice a melancholy ragtime song. No doubt a fire was now lit in the corner near the wall, my sleeping place, and Bill Teake was there preparing a mess-tin of tea.

The hour was twilight, the hour of early stars and early star-shells, of dreams and fancies and longings for home. It is then that all objects take on strange shapes, when every jutting traverse becomes alive with queer forms, the stiff sandbag becomes a gnome, the old dug-out, leaning wearily on its props, an ancient crone, spirits lurk in every nook and corner of shadows; the sleep-heavy eyes of weary men see strange visions in the dark alleys of war. I entered the dugout. A little candle in a winding sheet flared dimly in a niche which I had cut in the wall a few days previous. Pryor was sitting on the floor, his hands clasped round his knees, and he was looking into infinite distances. Bill Teake was there, smoking a cigarette and humming his ragtime tune. Two other soldiers were there, lying on the floor and probably asleep. One was covered with a blanket, but his face was bare, a sallow face with a blue, pinched nose, a weak, hairy jaw, and an open mouth that gaped at the rafters. The other man lay at his feet, breathing heavily. No fire was lit as yet.

"No rations have arrived?" I asked.

"No blurry rations," said Bill. "Never no rations now, nothink now at all. I 'ad a loaf yesterday and I left it in my pack in the trench, and when I come to look for't, it was gone."

"Who took it?" I asked.

"Ask me another!" said Bill with crushing irony. "'Oo ate the first bloater? Wot was the size of my great grandmuvver's boots when she was twenty-one? But '00 pinched my loaf? and men in this crush that would pinch a dead mouse from a blind kitten! Yer do ask some questions, Pat!"

"Bill and I were having a discussion a moment ago," said Pryor, interrupting. "Bill maintains that the Army is not an honourable institution, and that no man should join it. If he knew as much as he knowf nw he would neve/have come into it. I was saying, that"

"Oh, you were talkin' through yer ""at, that's wot you were," said Bill. "The harmy a place of honour indeed! 'Oo wants to join it now? Nobody as far as I can see. The married men say to the single men, 'You go and fight, you slackers! We'll stay at 'ome; we 'ave our old women to keep!' Sayin' that, the swine!" said Bill angrily. "Them thinkin' that the single men 'ave nothin' to do but to go out and fight for other men's wives. Blimey! that ain't 'arf cheek!"

"That doesn't alter the fact that our cause is just," said Pryor. "The Lord God of Hosts is with us yet, and the Church says that all men should fight—except clergymen."

"And why shouldn't them parsons fight?" asked Bill. "They say, 'Go and God bless you' to us, and then they won't fight themselves. It's against the laws of God, they say. If we 'ad all the clergymen, all the M.P.'s, the Kaiser and Crown Prince, Krupp and von Kluck, and all these 'ere blokes wot tell us to fight, in these 'ere trenches for a week, the war would come to an end very sudden."

Pryor rose and tried to light a fire. Wood was very scarce, the paper was wet and refused to burn.

"No fire to-night," said Bill in a despondent voice. "Two pieces of wood on a brazier is no go; they look like two crossbones on a 'earse."

"Are rations coming up to-night?" I asked. The ration wagons had been blown to pieces on the road the night before and we were very' hungry now.

"I suppose our grub will get lost this night again," said Bill. "It's always the way. I wish I was shot like that bloke there."

"Where?" I asked.

"There," answered Bill, pointing at the man with the blue and pinched face who lay in the corner. "'E's gone West."

"No," I said. "He's asleep!"

"'E'll not get up at revelly, 'im,'" said Bill. "'E's out of the doin's for good. 'E got wounded at the door and we took 'im in. 'E died."...

I approached the prostrate figure, examined him, and found that Bill spoke the truth.

"A party has gone down to Maroc for rations," said Pryor, lighting a cigarette and puffing the smoke up towards the roof. "They'll be back by eleven, I hope. That's if they're not blown to pieces. A lot of men got hit going down last night, and then there was no grub when they got to the dumping ground."

"This man," I said, pointing to the snoring figure on the ground. "He is all right?"

"Dead beaf: only," said Pryor; "but otherwise safe. I am going to have a kip now if I can."

So saying he bunched up against the wall, leant his elbow on the brazier that refused to burn, and in a few seconds he was fast asleep. Bill and I lay down together, keeping as far away as we could from the dead man, and did our best to snatch a few minutes' repose. that he was dead. I tried to prove to him that it was not quite the right and proper thing to do, to walk when life had left the body. But he paid not a sign of heed to my declamation. In the open space between our line and that of the Germans the dead man halted and told me to dig a grave for him there. A shovel came into my hand by some strange means and I set to work with haste; if the Germans saw me there they would start to shell me. The sooner I got the job done the better.

We nestled close to the muddy floor across which the shadows of the beams and sandbags crept in ghostly play. Now the shadows bunched into heaps, again they broke free, lacing and interlacing as the lonely candle flared from its niche in the wall.

The air light and rustling was full of the scent of wood smoke from a fire ablaze round the traverse, of the smell of mice, and the soft sounds and noises of little creeping things.

Shells travelling high in air passed over our dug-out; the Germans were shelling the Loos Road and the wagons that were coming along there. Probably that one just gone over had hit the ration wagon. The light of the candle failed and died: the night full of depth and whispering warmth swept into the dug-out, cloaked the sleeping and the dead, and settled, black and ghostly, in the corners. I fell asleep.

Bill tugging at my tunic awoke me from a horrible nightmare. In my sleep I had gone with the dead man from the hut out into the open. He walked with me, the dead man, who knew

"Deep?" I asked the man when I had laboured for a space. There was no answer. I looked up 1 at the place where he stood to find the man gone. On the ground was a short white stump of bone. This I was burying when Bill shook me.

"Rations 'ave come, Pat," he said.

"What's the time now?" I asked, getting to my feet and looking round. A fresh candle had been lit; the dead man still lay in the corner, but Pryor was asleep in the blanket.

"About midnight," said my mate, "or maybe a bit past. Yer didn't 'arf 'ave a kip."

"I was dreaming," I said. "Thought I was burying a man between the German lines."

"You'll soon be burying a man or two," said Bill.

"Who are to be buried?" I asked.

"The ration party."

"What!"

"The men copped it comin' up 'ere," said Bill. "Three of 'em were wiped out complete. The others escaped. I went out with Murney and O'Meara and collared the grub. I'm just goin' to light a fire now."

"I'll help you," I said, and began to cut a fresh supply of wood which had come from nowhere in particular with my clasp-knife.

A fire was soon burning merrily, a messtin of water was singing, and Bill had a few slices of bacon on the messtin lid ready to go on the brazier when the tea came off.

"This is wot I call comfy," he said. "Gawd, I'm not 'arf 'ungry. I could eat an 'oss."

I took off the tea, Bill put the lid over the flames and in a moment the bacon was sizzling.

"Where's the bread, Bill?" I asked.

"In that there sandbag," said my mate, pointing to a bag beside the door.

I opened the bag and brought out the loaf. It felt very moist. I looked at it and saw that it was coloured dark red.

"What's this?" I asked.

"Wot?" queried Bill, kicking Pryor to waken him.

"This bread has a queer colour," I said. "See it, Pryor."

Pryor gazed at it with sleep-heavy eyes.

"It's red," he muttered.

"Its colour is red," I said.

"Red," said Bill. "Well, we're damned 'ungry any'ow. I'd eat it if it was covered with rat poison."

"How did it happen?" I asked.

"Well, it's like this," said Bill. "The bloke as was carryin' it got 'it in the chest. The rations fell all round 'im and 'e fell on top of 'em. That's why the loaf is red."

We were very hungry, and hungry men,are not fastidious.

We made a good meal.

When we had eaten we went out and buried the dead.

CHAPTER XVII MICHAELMAS EVE

It's "Carry on!" and "Carry on I" and "Carry on!" all day,
And when we cannot carry on, they'll carry us away
To slumber sound beneath the ground, pore beggars dead
. and gone,
'Til Gabriel shouts on Judgment Day, "Get out and carry on!"

N Michaelmas Eve things were quiet; the big guns were silent, and the only sign of war was in the star-shells playing near Hill 70; the rifles pinging up by Bois Hugo, and occasional clouds of shrapnel incense which the guns offered to the god they could not break, the Tower Bridge of Loos. We had not been relieved yet, but we hoped to get back to Les Brebis for a rest shortly. The hour was midnight, and I felt very sleepy. The wounded in our sector had been taken in, the peace of the desert was over the level land and its burden of unburied dead. I put on my overcoat, one that I had just found in a pack on the roadway, and went into a barn which stood near our trench. The door of the building hung on one hinge. I pulled it off, placed it on the floor, and lay on it. With due caution I lit a cigarette, and the smoke reeked whitely upwards to the skeleton roof which the shell fire had stripped of nearly all its tiles.

My body was full of delightful pains of weariness, my mind was full of contentment. The moon struggled through a rift in the clouds and a shower of pale light streamed through the chequered framework overhead. The tiles which had weathered a leaden storm showed dark against the sky, queer shadows played on the floor, and in the subdued moonlight, strange, unexpected contrasts were evoked. In the corners, where the shadows took on definite forms, there was room for the imagination to revel in. The night of ruination with its soft moonlight and delicate shading had a wonderful fascination of its own. The enemy machine gun, fumbling for an opening, chirruped a lullaby as its bullets pattered against the wall. I was under the spell of an enchanting poem. "How good, how very good it is to be alive," I said.

My last remembrance before dozing off was of the clatter of picks and shovels on the road outside. The sanitary squad was at work burying the dead. I fell asleep.

I awoke to find somebody tugging at my elbow and to hear a voice which I recognised as W.'s, saying, "It's only old Pat."

"What's wrong?" I mumbled, raising myself on my elbow and looking round. The sanitary diggers were looking at me, behind them the Twin Towers stood out dark against the moonlight. Girders, ties and beams seemed to have been outlined with a pen dipped in molten silver. I was out in the open.

"This isn't half a go," said one of the men, a mate of mine, who belonged to the sanitary squad. "We thought you were a dead 'un. We dug a deep grave, put two in and there was room for another. Then L,. said that there»was a bloke lying on a door inside that house, and in we goes and carries you out—door and all. You're just on the brink of your grave now."

I peeped over the side and down a dark hole with a bundle of khaki and a white face at the bottom.

"I refuse to be buried," I muttered, and took up my bed and walked.

As I lay down again in the building which I had left to be buried, I could hear my friends laughing. It was a delightful joke. In a moment I was sound asleep.

I awoke with a start to a hell-riot of creaking timbers and tiles falling all around me. I got to my feet and crouched against the wall shuddering, almost paralyzed with fear. A tense second dragged by. The tiles ceased to fall and I looked up at the place where the roof had been. But the roof was gone; a shell had struck the centre beam, raised the whole construction as a lid is raised from a teapot, and flung it over into the street.... I rushed out into the trench in undignified haste, glad of my miraculous escape from death, and stumbled across Bill Teake as I fell into the trench.

"Wot's wrong with yer, mate?" he asked.

I drew in a deep breath and was silent for a moment. I was trying to regain my composure.

"Bill," I replied, "this is the feast of St. Michael and All Angels. I've led such an exemplary life that St. Michael and All Angels in Paradise want me to visit them. They caused the sanitary squad to dig my grave to-night, and when I refused to be buried they sent a shell along to strafe me. I escaped. I refuse to be virtuous from now until the end of my days."

"'Ave a drop of rum, Pat," said Bill, uncorking a bottle.

"Thank you, Bill," I said, and drank. I wiped my lips.

"Are we going to be relieved?" I asked.

"In no time," said Bill. "The 22nd London are coming along the trench now. We're going back to L,es Brebis."

"Good," I said.

"'Ave another drop of rum," said Bill.

He left me then and I began to make up my pack. It was useless for me to wait any longer. I would go across the fields to Les Brebis.

The night grew very dark, and heavy clouds gathered overhead. The nocturnal rustling of the field surrounded me, the dead men lay everywhere and anyhow, some head-downwards in shell-holes, others sitting upright as they were caught by a fatal bullet when dressing their wounds. Many were spread out at full length, their legs close together, their arms extended, crucifixes fashioned from decaying flesh wrapped in khaki. Nature, vast and terrible, stretched out on all sides; a red star-shell in the misty heavens looked like a lurid wound dripping with blood.

I walked slowly, my eyes fixed steadily on the field ahead, for I did not desire to trip over the dead, who lay everywhere. As I walked a shell whistled over my head and burst against the Twin Towers, and my gaze rested on the explosion. At that moment I tripped on something soft and went headlong across it. A dozen rats slunk away into the darkness.as I fell. I got to my feet again and looked at the dead man. The corpse was a mere condensation of shadows with a blurred though definite outline. It was a remainder and a reminder; a remnant of clashing steel, of rushing figures, of loud-voiced imprecations—of war, a reminder of mad passion, of or-' ganised hatred, of victory and defeat.

Engirt with the solitude and loneliness of the night it wasted away, though no waste could alter it now; it was a man who was not; henceforth it would be that and that alone.

For the thing there was not the quietude of death and the privacy of the tomb, it was outcast from its kind. Buffeted by the breeze, battered by the rains it rotted in the open. Worms feasted on its entrails, slugs trailed silverly over its face, and lean rats gnawed at its flesh. The air was full of the thing, the night stank with its decay. «

Life revolted at that from which life was gone, the quick cast it away for it was not of them. The corpse was one with the mystery of the night, the darkness and the void.

In Loos the ruined houses looked gloomy by day, by night they were ghastly. A house is a ruin when the family that dwelt within its walls is gone; but by midnight in the waste, how horrible looks the house of flesh from which the soul is gone. We are vaguely aware of what has happened when we look upon the tenantless home, but man is stricken dumb when he sees the tenantless body of one of his kind. I could only stare at the corpse until I felt thatmy eyes were as glassy as those on which I gazed. The stiffness of the dead was communicated to my being, the silence was infectious; I hardly dared to breathe.

"This is the end of all the mad scurry and rush," I said. "What purpose does it serve? And why do I stand here looking at the thing?" There were thousands of dead around Loos; fifty thousand perhaps, scattered over a few square miles of country, unburied. Some men, even, might still be dying.

A black speck moved along the earth a few yards away from me, slunk up to the corpse and disappeared into it, as it were. Then another speck followed, and another. The rats were returning to their meal.

The bullets whistled past my ears. The Germans had a machine gun and several fixed rifles trained on the Valle cross-roads outside Loos, and all night long these messengers of death sped out to meet the soldiers coming up the road and chase the soldiers going down.

The sight of the dead man and the rats had shaken me; I felt nervous and could not restrain myself from looking back over my shoulder at intervals. I had a feeling that something was following me, a Presence, vague and terrible, a spectre of the midnight and the field of death.

I am superstitious after a fashion, and I fear the solitude of the night and the silent obscurity of the darkness.

Once, at Vermelles, I passed through a deserted trench in the dusk. There the parapet and parados were fringed with graves, and decrepit dug-outs leant wearily on their props like hags on crutches. A number of the dug-outs had fallen in, probably on top of the sleeping occupants, and no one had time to dig the victims out. Such things often happen in the trenches, and in wet weather when the sodden dug-outs cave in, many men are buried alive.

The trench wound wayward as a river through the fields, its traverse steeped in shadow, its bays full of mystery. As I walked through the maze my mind was full of presentiments of evil. I was full of expectation, everything seemed to be leading up to happenings weird and uncanny, things which would not be of this world. The trench was peopled with spectres; soldiers, fully armed, stood on the fire-steps, their faces towards the enemy. I could see them as I entered a bay, but on coming closer the phantoms died away. The boys in khaki were tilted sandbags heaped on the banquette, the bayonets splinters of wood sharply defined against the sky. As if to heighten the illusion, torn ground-sheets, hanging from the parados, made sounds like travelling shells, as the breezes caught them and brushed them against the wall.

I went into a bay to see something dark grey and shapeless bulked in a heap on the fire-step. Another heap of sandbags I thought. But no! In the darkness of the weird locality realities were exaggerated and the heap which I thought was a large one was in reality very small; a mere soldier, dead in the trench, looked enormous in my eyes. The man's bayonet was pressed between his elbow and side, his head bending forward almost touched the knees, and both the man's hands were clasped across it as if for protection. A splinter of shell which he stooped to avoid must have caught him. He now was the sole occupant of the deserted trench, this poor, frozen effigy of fear. The trench was a grave unfilled.... I scrambled over the top and took my way across the open towards my company.

Once, at midnight, I came through the deserted village of Bully-Grenay, where every house was built exactly like its neighbour. War has played havoc with the pattern, however, most of the houses are shell-stricken, and some are levelled to the ground. The church stands on a little knoll near the coal-mine, and a shell has dug a big hole in the floor of the aisle. A statue of the Blessed Virgin sticks head downwards in the hole; how it got into this ludicrous position is a mystery.

The Germans were shelling the village as I came through. Shrapnel swept the streets and high explosives played havoc with the mine; I had no love for a place in such a plight. In front of me a limber was smashed to pieces, the driver was dead, the offside wheeler dead, the nearside wheeler dying and kicking its mate in the belly with vicious hooves. On either side of me were deserted houses with the doors open and shadows brooding in the interior. The cellars would afford secure shelter until the row was over, but I feared the darkness and the gloom more than I feared the shells in the open street. When the splinters swept perilously near to my head I made instinctively for an open door, but the shadows seemed to thrust me back with a powerful hand. To save my life I would not go into a house and seek refuge in the cellars.

I fear the solitude of the night, but I can never ascertain what it is I fear in it. I am not particularly interested in the supernatural, and spiritualism and table-rapping is not at all to my taste. In a crowded room a spirit in my way of thinking loses its dignity and power to impress, and at times I am compelled to laugh at those who believe in manifestations of disembodied spirits.

Once, at Givenchy, a soldier in all seriousness spoke of a strange sight which he had seen. Givenchy Church has only one wall standing, and a large black crucifix with its nailed Christ is fixed to this wall. From the trenches on a moonlight night it is possible to see the symbol of sorrow with its white figure which seems to keep eternal watch over the line of battle. The soldier of whom I speak was on guard; the night was very clear, and the enemy were shelling Givenchy Church. A splinter of shell knocked part of the arm of the cross away. The soldier on watch vowed that he saw a luminous halo settle round the figure on the Cross. It detached itself from its nails, came down to the ground, and put the fallen wood back to its place. Then the Crucified resumed His exposed position again on the, Cross. It was natural that the listeners should say that the sentry was drunk.

It is strange how the altar of Givenchy Church and its symbol of Supreme Agony has escaped destruction. Many crosses in wayside shrines have been untouched though the locality in which they stand is swept with eternal artillery fire.

But many have fallen; when they become one with the rubble of a roadway their loss is unnoticed. It is when they escape destruction that they become conspicuous. They are like the faithful in a storm at sea who prayed to the Maria del Stella and weathered the gale. Their good fortune became common gossip. But gossip, historical and otherwise, is mute upon those who perished.

CHAPTER XVIII BACK AT LOOS

The dead men lay on the shell-scarred plain,
Where death and the autumn held their reign-
Like banded ghosts in the heavens grey
The smoke of the conflict died away.
The boys whom I knew and loved were dead,
Where war's grim annals were writ in red,
In the town of Loos in the morning.

THE ruined village lay wrapped in the silence of death. It was a corpse over which the stars came out like funeral tapers. The star-shells held the heaven behind Loos, forming into airy constellations which vanished at a breath. The road, straight as an arrow, pitted with shell-holes and bearing an incongruous burden of dead mules, dead men, broken limbers, and vehicles of war, ran in front of us straight up to and across the firing line into the France that was not France. Out there behind the German lines were the French villagers and peasantry, fearing any advance on our part, much more even than the Germans feared it, even as much as the French behind our lines feared a German advance.

The indefatigable shrapnel kills impartially; how many civilians in Loos and Lens have fallen victims to the furious 75's? In France the Allies fight at a disadvantage; a few days previously a German ammunition depot had been blown up in Lille, and upwards of a hundred French civilians were killed. How much more effective it would have been if the civilians had been Germans!

Our battalion was returning to the trenches after a fortnight's rest in H, a village in the rear. We had handed over the trench taken from the Germans to the 22nd London Regiment before leaving for H. In H we got a new equipment, fresh clothing, good boots and clean shirts; now we were ready for further work in active warfare.

We were passing through Loos on the way to the trenches. What a change since we had been there last! The adaptive French had taken the village in hand; they had now been there for three days. Three days, and a miracle had been accomplished. Every shell-crater in the street was filled up with dead horses, biscuit tins, sandbags and bricks, and the place was made easy for vehicle traffic. Barricades, behind which machine guns lurked privily, were built at the main crossings. An old bakery was patched up and there bread was baked for the soldiers. In a cellar near the square a neat wine-shop displayed tempting bottles which the thirsty might purchase for a few sous.

The ease with which the French can accommodate themselves to any change has been a constant source of wonder to me. In Les Brebis I saw roofs blown off the village houses at dawn, at noon I saw the natives putting them on again; at Cuinchy I saw an ancient woman selling *cafeau-lait* at four sous a cup in the jumble of bricks which was once her home. When the cow which supplied the milk was shot in the stomach the woman still persisted in selling coffee, *cafe noir*, at three sous a cup. When a civilian is killed at Mazingarbe the children of the place sell the percussion cap of the death-dealing shell for half a franc. Once when I was there an old crone was killed when washing her feet at a street pump. A dozen or more percussion caps were sold that day; every *gargon* in the neighbourhood claimed that the aluminium nose-cap in his possession was the one that did the foul deed. When I was new to France I bought several of these ghastly relics, but in a few weeks I was out trying to sell. There was then, however, a slump in nose-caps, and I lost heavily.

The apt process of accommodation which these few incidents may help to illustrate is peculiar to the French; they know how to make the best of a bad job and a ruined village. They paved the streets with dead horses; drew bread from the bricks and stored wine in the litter that was Loos. That is France, the Phœnix that rises resplendent from her ashes; France that like her Joan of Arc will live for ever because she has suffered; France, a star, like Rabelais, which can cast aside a million petty vices when occasion requires it and glow with eternal splendour, the wonder of the world.

The Munster Fusiliers held a trench on the left of Loos and they had suffered severely. They had been in there for eight days, and the big German guns were active all the time. In one place the trench was filled in for a distance of three hundred yards. Think of what that means. Two hundred men manned the deep, cold alley dug in the clay. The shells fell all round the spot, the parados swooped forward, the parapet dropped back, they were jaws which devoured men. The soldiers went in there, into a grave that closed like a trap. None could escape. When we reopened the trench, we reopened a grave and took out the dead.

The night we came to relieve those who remained alive was clear and the stars stood out cold and brilliant in the deep overhead; but a grey haze enveloped the horizon, and probably we would have rain before the dawn. The trenches here were dug recently, makeshift alleys they were, insecure and muddy, lacking dugouts, fire-places, and every accommodation that might make a soldier's life bearable. They were fringed with dead; dead soldiers in khaki lay on the reverse slope of the parapet, their feet in the grass, their heads on the sandbags; they lay behind the parados, on the levels, in the woods, everywhere. Upwards of eleven thousand English dead littered the streets of Loos and the country round after the victory, and many of these were unburied yet.

A low-lying country, wet fields, stagnant drains, shell-rent roads, ruined houses, dead men, mangled horses. To us soldiers this was the only apparent result of the battle of Loos, a battle in which we fought at the start, a battle which was not yet ended. We knew nothing of the bigger issues of the fight. We had helped to capture several miles of trenches and a few miles of country. We brought our guns forward, built new emplacements, to find that the enemy knew his abandoned territory so well that he easily located the positions of our batteries. Before the big fight our guns round Les Brebis and Maroc were practically immune from observation; now they were shelled almost as soon as they were placed. We thrust our salient forward like a duck's bill, and our trenches were subject to enfilade fire and in some sectors our men were even shelled from the rear.

Our plan of attack was excellent, our preparations vigorous and effective, as far as they went. Our artillery blew the barbed wire entanglements of the first German trench to pieces, at the sec ond trench the wire was practically untouched.

Our regiment entered this latter trench where it runs along in front of Loos. We followed on the heels of the retreating Germans. Our attack might have been more effective if the real offensive began here, if fresh troops were flung at the disorganised Germans when the second trench was taken. Lens might easily have fallen into our hands.

The fresh divisions coming up on Sunday and Monday had to cope with the enemy freshly but strongly entrenched on Hill 70. The Guards Division crossed from Maroc in open order on the afternoon of Sunday, the 26th, and was greeted by a furious artillery fire which must have worked great havoc amongst the men. I saw the advance from a distance. I think it was the most imposing spectacle of the fight. What struck me as very strange at the time was the Division crossing the open when they might have got into action by coming along through the trenches. On the level the men were under observation all the time. The advance, like that of the London Irish, was made at a steady pace.

What grand courage it is that enables men to face the inevitable with untroubled front. Despite the assurance given by the Higher Command about the easy task in front of us, the boys of our regiment, remembering Givenchy and Richebourg, gave little credence to the assurance; they anticipated a very strong resistance, in fact none of them hoped to get beyond the first German trench.

It is easy to understand why men are eager "to get there," as the favourite phrase says, once they cross the parapet of the assembly trench. "There," the enemy's line, is comparatively safe, and a man can dodge a blow or return one. The open offers no shelter; between the lines luck alone preserves a man; a soldier is merely a naked babe pitted against an armed gladiator. Naturally he wants "to get there" with the greatest possible speed; in the open he is beset with a thousand dangers, in the foeman's trench he is confronted with but one or two.

I suppose "the desire to get there," which is so often on the lips of the military correspondent, is as often misconstrued. The desire to get finished with the work is a truer phrase. None wish to go to a dentist, but who would not be rid of an aching tooth?

The London Irish advance was more remarkable than many have realized. The instinct of self-preservation is the strongest in created beings, and here we see hundreds of men whose premier consideration was their own personal safety moving forward to attack with the nonchalance of a church parade. Perhaps the men who kicked the football across were the most nervous in the affair. Football is an exciting pastime, it helped to take the mind away from the crisis ahead, and the dread anticipation of death was forgotten for the time being. But I do not think for a second that the ball was brought for that purpose.

Although we captured miles of trenches, the attack in several parts stopped on open ground where we had to dig ourselves in. This necessitated much labour and afforded little comfort. Dug-outs there were none, and the men who occupied the trenches after the fight had no shelter from shell-splinters and shrapnel. From trenches such as these we relieved all who were left of the Munster Fusiliers.

The Germans had placed some entanglements in front of their position, and it was considered necessary to examine their labours and see what they had done. If we found that their wire entanglement was strong and well fastened our conclusions would be that the Germans were not ready to strike, that their time at the moment was devoted to safeguarding themselves from attack. If, on the other hand, their wires were light, fragile and easily removed, we might guess that an early offensive on our lines would take place. Lieutenant Y. and two men went across to have a look at the enemy's wires; we busied j ourselves digging a deeper trench; as a stretcherbearer I had no particular work for the moment, so I buried a few of the dead who lay on the field.

On our right was a road which crossed our trench and that of the Germans, a straight road lined with shell-scarred poplars running true as an arrow into the profundities of the unknown. The French occupied the trench on our right, and a gallant Porthos (I met him later) built a barricade of sand-bags on the road, and sitting there all night with a fixed rifle, he fired bullet after bullet down the highway. His game was to hit cobbles near the German trenches, from there the bullet went splattering and ricochetting, hopping and skipping along the road for a further five hundred yards, making a sound like a pebble clattering down the tiles of a roof. Many a Boche coming along that road must have heartily cursed the energetic Porthos.

Suddenly the report of firearms came from the open in front, then followed two yells, loud and agonising, and afterwards silence. What had happened? Curiosity prompted me to rush into the trench, leaving a dead soldier half buried, and make inquiries. All the workers had ceased their labour, they stood on the fire-steps staring into the void in front of them, their ears tensely strained. Something must have happened to the patrol, probably the officer and two men had been surprised by the enemy and killed....

As we watched, three figures suddenly emerged from the greyness in front, rushed up to the parapet, and flung themselves hastily into the trench. The listening patrol had returned. Breathlessly they told a story.

They had examined the enemy's wire and were on the way back when one of the men stumbled into a shell-hole on the top of three Germans who were probably asleep. The Boches scrambled to their feet and faced the intruders. The officer fired at one and killed him instantly, one of our boys ran another through the heart with the bayonet, the third German got a crack on the head with a rifle-butt and collapsed, yelling. Then the listening patrol rushed hurriedly in, told their story and consumed extra tots of rum when the exciting narrative was finished.

The morning country was covered with white fogs; Bois Hugo, the wood on our left, stood out an island in a sea of milk. Twenty yards away from the trench was the thick whiteness, the unknown. Our men roamed about the open picking up souvenirs and burying dead. Probably in the mist the Germans were at work, too.... All was very quiet, not a sound broke the stillness, the riot of war was choked, suffocated, in the cold, soft fog.

All at once an eager breeze broke free and swept across the parapet, driving the fog away. In the space of five seconds the open was bare, the cloak which covered it was swept off. Then we saw many things.

Our boys in khaki came rushing back to their trench, flinging down all souvenirs in their haste to reach safety; the French on our right scampered to their burrows, casting uneasy eyes behind them as they ran. A machine gun might open and play havoc. Porthos had a final shot down the road, then he disappeared and became one with the field.

But the enemy raced in as we did; their indecorous haste equalled ours. They had been out, too. One side retreated from the other, and none showed any great gallantry in the affair. Only when the field was clear did the rifles speak. Then there was a lively ten minutes and a few thousand useless rounds were wasted by the combatants before they sat down to breakfast.

"A strategic retreat," said Pryor. "I never ran so quickly in all my life. I suppose it is like this every night, men working between the lines, engineers building entanglements, covering parties sleeping out their watch, listening patrols and souvenir hunters doing their little bit in their own particular way. It's a funny way of conducting a war." "It's strange," I said.

"We have no particular hatred for the men across the way," said Pryor. "My God, the trenches tone a man's temper. When I was at home (Pryor had just had ten days' furlough) our drawing-room bristled with hatred of some being named the Hun. Good Heavens! you should hear the men past military age revile the Hun. If they were out here we couldn't keep them from getting over the top to have a smack at the foe. And the women! If they were out here, they would just simply tear the Germans to pieces. I believe that we are the wrong men, we able-bodied youths with even tempers. It's the men who are past military age who should be out here."

Pryor was silent for a moment.

"I once read a poem, a most fiery piece of verse," he continued; "and it urged all men to take part in the war, get a gun and get off to Flanders immediately. Shame on those who did not go! The fellow who wrote that poem is a bit of a literary swell, and I looked up his name in 'Who's Who,' and find that he is a year or two above military age. If I were a man of seventy and could pick up fury enough to write that poem, I'd be off to the recruiting agent the moment the last line was penned, and I'd tell the most damnable lies to get off and have a smack at the Hun. But that literary swell hasn't enlisted yet." A pause.

"And never will," Pryor concluded, placing a mess-tin of water on a red-hot brazier. Breakfast would be ready shortly.

CHAPTER XIX WOUNDED

"if you're lucky you'll get killed quick; if you're damned lucky you'll get 'it where it don't 'urt, and sent back to Blighty."—Bill Teake's Philosophy.

SOME min have all the damned luck that's agoin'," said Corporal Flaherty. "There's Murney, and he's been at home two times since he came out here. Three months ago he was allowed to go home and see his wife and to welcome a new Murney into the wurl'. Then in the Loos do the other day he got a bit of shrapnel in his heel and now he's home again. I don't seem to be able to get home at all. I wish I had got Murney's shrapnel in my heel.... I'm sick of the trenches; I wish the war was over."

"What were you talking to the Captain about yesterday?" asked Rifleman Barty, and he winked knowingly.

"What the devil is it to you?" inquired Flaherty.

"It's nothin' at all to me," said Barty. "I would just like to know."

"Well, you'll not know," said the Corporal.

"Then maybe I'll be allowed to make a guess," said Barty. "You'll not mind me guessin', will yer?"

"Hold your ugly jaw!" said Flaherty, endeavouring to smile, but I could see an uneasy look in the man's eyes. "Ye're always blatherin'."

"Am I?" asked Barty, and turned to us. "Corp'ril Flaherty," he said, "is goin' home on leave to see his old woman and welcome a new Flaherty into the world, just like Murney did three months ago."

Flaherty went red in the face, then white. He fixed a killing look on Barty and yelled at him: "Up you get on the fire-step and keep on sentry till I tell ye ye're free. That'll be a damned long time, me boy!"

"You're a gay old dog, Flaherty," said Barty, making no haste to obey the order. "One wouldn't think that there was so much in you; isn't that so, my boys? Papa Flaherty wants to get home!"

Barty winked again and glanced at the men who surrounded him. There were nine of us there altogether; sardined in the bay of the trench which the Munster Fusiliers held a few days ago. Nine! Flaherty, whom I knew very well, a Dublin man with a wife in London, Barty a Cockney of Irish descent, the Cherub, a stout youth with a fresh complexion, soft red lips and tender blue eyes, a sergeant, a very good fellow and kind to his men.... The others I knew only slightly, one of them a boy of nineteen or twenty had just come out from England; this was his second day in the trenches.

The Germans were shelling persistently all the morning, but missing the trench every time. They were sending big stuff across, monster 9/2 shells which could not keep pace with their own sound; we could hear them panting in from the unknown—three seconds before they had crossed our trench to burst in Bois Hugo, the wood at the rear of our line. Big shells can be seen in air, and look to us like beer bottles whirling in space; some of the men vowed they got thirsty when they saw them. Lighter shells travel more quickly: we only become aware of these when they burst; the boys declare that these messengers of destruction have either got rubber heels or stockinged soles.

"I wish they would stop 'this shelling," said the Cherub in a low, patient voice. He was a good boy, he loved everything noble and he had a generous sympathy for all his mates. Yes, and even for the men across the way who were enduring the same hardships as himself in an alien trench.

"You know, I get tired of these trenches sometimes," he said diffidently. "I wish the war was over and done with."

I went round the traverse into another bay less crowded, sat down on the fire-step and began to write a letter. I had barely written two words when a shell in stockinged soles burst with a vicious snarl, then another came plonk!... A shower of splinters came whizzing through the air.... Round the corner came a man walking hurriedly, unable to run because of a wound in the leg; another followed with a lacerated cheek, a third came along crawling on hands and knees and sat down opposite on the floor of the trench.

How lucky to have left the bay was my first thought, then I got to my feet and looked at the man opposite. It was Barty.

"Where did you get hit?" I asked.

"There!" he answered, and pointed at his boot which was torn at the toecap. "I was just going to look over the top when the shell hit and a piece had gone right through my foot near the big toe. I could hear it breaking through; it was like a dog crunching a bone. Gawd! it doesn't 'arf give me gip!"

I took the man's boot off and saw that the splinter of shell had gone right through, tearing tendons and breaking bones. I dressed the wound.

"There are others round there," an officer, coming up, said to me. I went back to the bay to find it littered with sandbags and earth, the parapet had been blown in. In the wreckage I saw Flaherty, dead; the Cherub, dead, and five others disfigured, bleeding and lifeless. Two shells had burst on the parapet, blew the structure in and killed seven men. Many others had been wounded; those with slight injuries hobbled away, glad to get free from the place, boys who were badly hurt lay in the clay and chalk, bleeding and moaning. Several stretcher-bearers had arrived and were at work dressing the wounds. High velocity shells were bursting in the open field in front, and shells of a higher calibre were hurling bushes and branches sky-high from Bois Hugo.

I placed Barty on my back and carried him down the narrow trench. Progress was difficult, and in places where the trench had been three parts filled with earth from bursting shells I had to crawl on all fours with the wounded man on my back. I had to move very carefully round sharp angles on the way; but, despite all precautions, the wounded foot hit against the wall several times. When this happened the soldier uttered a yell, then followed it up with a meek apology. "I'm sorry, old man; it did 'urt awful!"

Several times we sat down on the fire-step and rested. Once when we sat, the Brigadier-General came along and stopped in front of the wounded man.

"How do you feel?" asked the Brigadier.

"Not so bad," said the youth, and a wan smile flitted across his face. "It'll get me 'ome to England, I think."

"Of course it will," said the officer. "You'll be back in blighty in a day or two. Have you had any morphia?"

"No."

"Well, take two of these tablets," said the Brigadier, taking a little box from his pocket and emptying a couple of morphia pills in his hand. "Just put them under your tongue and allow them to dissolve.... Good luck to you, my boy!"

The Brigadier walked away; Barty placed the two tablets under his tongue.

"Now spit them out again," I said to Barty. "Why?" he asked.

"I've got to carry you down," I explained. "I use one arm to steady myself and the other to keep your wounded leg from touching the wall of the trench. You've got to grip my shoulders. Morphia will cause you to lose consciousness, and when that happens I can't carry you any further through this alley. You'll have to lie here till it's dark, when you can be taken across the open."

Barty spat out the morphia tablets and crawled upon my back again. Two stretcher-bearers followed me carrying a wounded man on a blanket, a most harrying business. The wounded man was bumping against the floor of the trench all the time, the stretcher-bearer in front had to walk backwards, the stretcher-bearer at rear was constantly tripping on the folds of the blanket. A mile of trench had to be traversed before the dressing-station was reached and it took the party two hours to cover that distance. An idea of this method of bringing wounded away from the firing-line may be gathered if you, reader, place a man in a blanket and, aided by a friend, carry him across the level floor of your drawing-room. Then, consider the drawing-room to be a trench, so narrow in many places that the man has to be turned on his side to get him through, and in other places so shaky that the slightest touch may cause parados and parapet to fall in on top of you.

For myself, except when a peculiar injury necessitates it, I seldom use a blanket. I prefer to place the wounded person prone on my back, get a comrade stretcher-bearer to hold his legs and thus crawl out of the trench with my burden. This, though trying on the knees, is not such a very difficult feat.

"How do you feel now, Barty?" I asked my comrade as we reached the door of the dressingstation.

"Oh, not so bad, you know," he answered. "Will the M.O. give me some morphia when we get in?"

"No doubt," I said.

I carried him in and placed him on a stretcher on the floor. At the moment the doctor was busy with another case.

"Chummy," said Barty, as I was moving away.

"Yes," I said, coming back to his side.

"It's like this, Pat," said the wounded boy. "I owe Corporal Darvy a 'arf-crown, Tubby Sinter two bob, and Jimmy James four packets of fags —woodbines. Will you tell them when you go back that I'll send out the money and fags when I go back to Mighty?"

"All right," I replied. "I'll let them know." CHAPTER XX FOR BLIGHTY

"The villa dwellers have become cave-dwellers."—Dudley Pryor. THE night was intensely dark, and from the door of the dug-out I could scarcely see the outline of the sentry who stood on the banquette fifteen yards away. Standing on tip-toe, I could glance over the parapet, and when a star-shell went up I could trace the outline of a ruined mill that stood up, gaunt and forbidding, two hundred yards away from our front line trench. On the left a line of shrapnel-swept trees stood up in air, leafless and motionless. Now and again a sniper's bullet hit the sandbags with a crack like a whip.

Lifeless bodies still lay in the trench; the blood of the wounded whom I had helped to carry down to the dressing-station was still moist on my tunic and trousers. In a stretch of eight hundred yards there was only one dug-out, a shaky construction, cramped and leaky, that might fall in at any moment.

"Would it be wise to light a fire?" asked Dilly, my mate, who was lying on the earthen floor of the dug-out. "I want a drop of tea. I didn't have a sup of tea all day."

"The officers won't allow us to light a fire," I said. "But if we hang a ground-sheet over the door the light won't get through. Is there a brazier?" I asked.

"Yes, there's one here," said Dilly. "I was just going to use it for a pillow, I feel so sleepy."

He placed a ground-sheet over the door while speaking and I took a candle from my pocket, lit it and placed it in a little niche in the wall. Then we split some wood with a clasp-knife, placed it on a brazier, and lit a fire over which we placed a mess-tin of water.

The candle flickered fitfully, and dark shadows lurked in the corners of the dug-out. A mouse peeped down from between the sandbags on the roof, its bright little eyes glowing with mischief. The ground-sheet hanging over the door was caught by a breeze and strange ripples played across it. We could hear from outside the snap of rifle bullets on the parapet....

"It's very quiet in here," said Dilly. "And I feel so like sleep. I hope none get hit to-night. I don't think I'd be able to help with a stretcher down to the dressing-station until I have a few hours' sleep.... How many wounded did we carry out to-day? Nine?"

"Nine or ten," I said.

"Sharney was badly hit," Dilly said. "I don't think he'll pull through."

"It's hard to say," I remarked, fanning the fire with a newspaper. "Felan, the cook, who was wounded in the charge a month ago, got a bullet in his shoulder. It came out through his back. I dressed his wound. It was ghastly. The bullet pierced his lung, and every time he breathed some of the air from the lung came out through his back. I prophesied that he would live for four or five hours. I had a letter from him the other day. He's in a London hospital and is able to walk about again. He was reported dead, too, in the casualty list."

"Some people pluck up wonderfully," said Dilly. "Is the tea ready?"

"It's ready," I said.

We sat down together, rubbing our eyes, for the smoke got into them, and opened a tin of bully beef. The beef with a few biscuits and a mess-tin of warm tea formed an excellent repast. When we had finished eating we lit our cigarettes.

"Have you got any iodine?" Dilly suddenly inquired.

"None," I answered. "Have you?"

"I got my pocket hit by a bullet coming up here," Dilly answered. "My bottle got smashed."

Iodine is so necessary when dressing wounds. Somebody might get hit during the night....

"I'll go to the dressing-station and get some," I said to Dilly. "You can have a sleep."

I put my coat on and went out, clambered up the rain-sodden parados and got out into the open where a shell-hole yawned at every step, and where the dead lay unburied. A thin mist lay low, and solitary trees stood up from a sea of milk, aloof, immobile. The sharp, penetrating stench of wasting flesh filled the air.

I suddenly came across two lone figures digging a hole in the ground. I stood still for a moment and watched them. One worked with a pick, the other with a shovel, and both men panted as they toiled. When a star-shell went up they threw themselves flat to earth and rose to resume their labours as the light died away.

Three stiff and rigid bundles wrapped in khaki lay on the ground near the diggers, and, having dug the hole deep and wide, the diggers turned to the bundles; tied a string round each in turn, pulled them forward and shoved them into the hole. Thus were three soldiers buried.

I stopped for a moment beside the grave.

"Hard at work, boys?" I said.

"Getting a few of them under," said one of the diggers. "By God, it makes one sweat, this work. Have you seen a dog about at all?" was the man's sudden inquiry.

"No," I answered. "I've heard about that dog. Is he not supposed to be a German in disguise?"

"He's old Nick in disguise," said the digger. "He feeds on the dead, the dirty swine. I don't like it all. Look! there's the dog again."

Something long, black and ghostly took shape in the mist ten yards away and stood there for a moment as if inspecting us. A strange thrill ran through my body.

"That's it again," said the nearest digger. "I've seen it three times to-night; once at dusk down by Loos graveyard among the tombstones, again eating a dead body, and now—some say it's a ghost."

I glanced at the man, then back again at the spot where the dog had been. But now the animal was gone.

An air of loneliness pervaded the whole place, the sounds of soft rustling swept along the ground: I could hear a twig snap, a man cough, and in the midst of all the little noises which merely accentuated the silence, it suddenly rose long-drawn and eerie, the howl of a lonely dog.

"The dirty swine," said the digger. "I wish somebody shot it."

"No one could shoot the animal," said the other worker. "It's not a dog; it's the devil himself."

My way took me past Loos church and churchyard; the former almost levelled to the ground, the latter delved by shells and the bones of the dead villagers flung broadcast to the winds of heaven. I looked at the graveyard and the white headstones. Here I saw the dog again. The silver light of a star-shell shot aslant a crumpled wall and enabled me to see a long black figure, noiseless as the shadow of a cloud, slink past the little stone crosses and disappear. Again a howl, lonely and weird, thrilled through the air.

I walked down the main street of Loos where dead mules lay silent between the shafts of their limbers. It was here that I saw Gilhooley die, Gilhooley the master bomber, Gilhooley the Irishman.,

"Those damned snipers are in thim houses up the street," he said, fingering a bomb lovingly. "But, by Jasus, we'll get them out of it." Then he was shot. This happened a month ago.

In the darkness the ruined houses assumed fantastic shapes, the fragment of a standing wall became a gargoyle, a demon, a monstrous animal. A hunchback leered down at me from a roof as I passed, his hump in air, his head thrust forward on knees that rose to his face. Further along a block of masonry became a gigantic woman who was stepping across the summit of a mountain, her shawl drawn over her head and a pitcher on her shoulder.

In the midst of the ruin and desolation of the night of morbid fancies, in the centre of a square lined with unpeopled houses, I came across the Image of Supreme Pain, the Agony of the Cross. What suffering has Loos known? What torture, what sorrow, what agony? The crucifix was well in keeping with this scene of desolation.

Old Mac of the R.A.M.C. was sitting on a blanket on the floor of the dressing-station when I entered. Mac is a fine singer and a hearty fellow; he is a great friend of mine.

"What do you want now?" he asked.

"A drop of rum, if you have any to spare," I answered.

"You're a devil for your booze," Mac said, taking the cork out of a water bottle which he often uses for an illegitimate purpose. "There's a wee drappie goin', man."

I drank.

"Not bad, a wee drappie," said Mac. "Ay, mon! it's health tae the navel and marrow to the bones."

"Are all the others in bed?" I asked. Several hands worked at the dressing-station, but Mac was the only one there now.

"They're having a wee bit kip down in the cellar," said Mac. "I'll get down there if you clear out."

"Give me some iodine, and I'll go," I said.

He filled a bottle, handed it to me, and I went out again to the street. A slight artillery row was in progress now, our gunners were shelling the enemy's trenches and the enemy were at work battering in our parapets.

A few high explosives were bursting at the Twin Towers of Loos and light splinters were singing through the air. Bullets were whizzing down the street and snapping at the houses. I lit a cigarette and smoked, concealing the glowing end under my curved fingers.

Something suddenly seemed to sting my wrist and a sharp pain shot up my arm. I raised my hand and saw a dark liquid dripping down my palm on to my fingers.

"I wonder if this will get me back to England," I muttered, and turned back to the dressing-station.

Mac had not gone down to the cellar; the water bottle was still uncorked.

"Back again?" he inquired.

"It looks like it," I replied.

"You're bleeding, Pat," he exclaimed, seeing the blood on my hand. "Strafed, you bounder, you're strafed."

He examined my wound and dressed it.

"Lucky dog," he said, handing me the water bottle. "You're for blighty, man, for blighty. I wish to God I was! Is it raining now?" he asked.

"It is just starting to come down," I said. "How am I to get out of this?" I inquired.

"There'll be an ambulance up here in a wee," Mac said, then he laughed. "Suppose it gets blown to blazes," he said.

"It's a quiet night," I remarked, but I was seized with a certain nervousness. "God! it would be awkward if I really got strafed now, on the way home."

"It often happens, man," said Mac, "and we are going to open all our guns on the enemy at two o'clock. They're mobilizing for an attack, it's said."

"At two o'clock," I repeated. "It's a quarter to two now. And it's very quiet."

"It'll not be quiet in a minute," said my friend.

I had a vivid impression. In my mind I saw the Germans coming up to their trench through the darkness, the rain splashing on their rifles and equipment, their forms bent under the weight which they carried. No doubt they had little bundles of firewood with them to cook their breakfasts at dawn. They were now thanking God that the night was quiet, that they could get into the comparative shelter of the trenches in safety. Long lines of men in grey, keeping close to the shelter of spinneys sunk in shadow; transport wagons rumbling and jolting, drivers unloading at the "dumps," ration parties crossing the open with burdens of eatables; men thinking of home and those they loved as they sat in their leaky dug-outs, scrawling letters by the light of their guttering candles. This was the life that went on in and behind the German lines in the darkness and rain.

Presently hell would burst open and a million guns would bellow of hatred and terror. I supposed the. dead on the fields would be torn and *t* ripped anew, and the shuddering quick out on the open where no discretion could preserve them and no understanding keep them, would plod nervously onward, fear in their souls and terror in their faces.

Our own men in the trenches would hear the 1 guns and swear at the gunners. The enemy would reply by shelling the trench in which our boys were placed. The infantry always suffers when Mars riots. All our guns would open fire.... It would be interesting to hear them speak.... I would remain here while the cannonade was on.. .. It would be safer and wiser to go than stay, but I would stay.

"Is there another ambulance besides the one due in a minute or two coming up before dawn, Mac?" I asked.

"Another at four o'clock," Mac announced sleepily. He lay on the floor wrapped in his blanket and was just dozing off.

"I'm finished with war for a few weeks at least," I muttered. "I'm pleased. I hope I get to England. Another casualty from Loos. The dead are lying all round here; civilians and soldiers. A dead child lying in a trench near Hulluch. I suppose somebody has buried it I wonder how it got there... . The line of wounded stretches from Lens to Victoria Station on this side, and from Lens to Berlin on the other side.... How many thousand dead are there in the fields round there?... There will be many more, for the battle of Loos is still proceeding.... Who is going to benefit by the carnage, save the rats which feed now as they have never fed before?... What has brought about this turmoil, this tragedy that cuts the heart of friend and foe alike?... Why have millions of men come here from all corners of Europe to hack and slay one another? What mysterious impulse guided them to this maiming, murdering, gouging, gassing, and filled them with such hatred? Why do we use the years of peace in preparation for war? Why do men well over the military age hate the Germans more than the younger and more sober souls in the trenches? Who has profited by this carnage? Who will profit? Why have some men joined in the war for freedom?"

Suddenly I was overcome with a fit of laughter, and old Mac woke up.

"What the devil are you kicking up such a row for?" he grumbled.

"Do you remember B, the fellow whose wound you dressed one night a week ago? Bald as a trout, double chin and a shrapnel wound in his leg. He belonged to the Regiment."

"I remember him," said Mac.

"I knew him in civil life," I said. "He kept a house of some repute in. The sons of the rich came there secretly at night; the poor couldn't afford to. Do you believe that B joined the Army in order to redress the wrongs of violated Belgium?"

Mat sat up on the floor, his Balaclava helmet pulled down over his ears, and winked at me.

"Ye're drunk, ye bounder, ye're drunk," he said. "Just like all the rest, mon. We'll have no teetotallers after the war."

He lay down again.

"I know a man who was out here for nine months and he never tasted drink," I said.

Mac sat up again, an incredulous look on his face.

"Who was he?" he asked.

"The corporal of our section," I replied.

"Well, that's the first I've heard o'," said Mac. "He's dead, isn't he?"

"Got killed in the charge," I answered. "I saw him coming back wounded, crawling along with his head to the ground like a dog scenting the trail."

Sleep was heavy in my eyes and queer thoughts ran riot in my head. "What is to be the end of this destruction and decay? That is what it means, this war. Destruction, decay, degradation. We who are here know its degradation; we, the villa dwellers, who have become cave dwellers and make battle with club and knobkerry; the world knows of the destruction and decay of war. Man will recognise its futility before he recognises its immorality.... Lines of men marching up long, poplar-lined roads to-day; to-morrow the world grows sick with their decay.... They are now one with Him.... Yes, there He is, hanging on the barbed wires. I shall go and speak to Him...."

The dawn blushed in the east and grew redder and redder like a curtain of blood—and from Souchez to Ypres the poppy fields were of the same red colour, a plain of blood. For miles and miles the barbed wire entanglements wound circuitously through the levels, brilliant with starclusters of dew-drops hung from spike, barb and intricate traceries of gossamer. Out in front of my bay gleamed the Pleiades which had dropped from heaven during the night and clustered round a dark grey bulk of clothing by one of the entanglement props. I knew the dark grey bulk, it was He; for days and nights He had hung there, a huddled heap; the Futility of War.

I was with Him in a moment endeavouring to help Him. In the dawn He was not repulsive, He was almost beautiful, but His beauty was that of the mirage which allures to a more sure destruction. The dew-drops were bright on His beard, His hair and His raiment; but His head sank low upon the wires and I could not see His face.

A dew-drop disappeared from the man's beard as I watched and then another. Round me the glory of the wires faded; the sun, coming out warm and strong, dispelled the illusion of the dawn; the galaxy faded, leaving but the rugged props, the ghastly wires and the rusty barbs nakedly showing in the poppy field.

I saw now that He was repulsive, abject, pitiful lying there, His face close to the wires, a thousand bullets in his head. Unable to resist the impulse I endeavoured to turn His face upward, but was unable; a barb had pierced His eye and stuck there, rusting in the socket from which sight was gone. I turned and ran away from the thing into the bay of the trench. The glory of the dawn had vanished, my soul no longer swooned in the ecstasy of it; the Pleiades had risen, sick of that which they decorated, the glorious disarray of jewelled dew-drops was no more, that which endured the full light of day was the naked and torturing contraption of war. Was not the dawn buoyant, like the dawn of patriotism? Were not the dew-decked wires war seen from far off? Was not He in wreath of Pleiades glorious death in action? But a ray of light more, and what is He and all with Him but the monstrous futility of war.... Mac tugged at my shoulder and I awoke.

"Has the shelling begun?" I asked.

"It's over, mon," he said. "It's four o'clock now. You'll be goin' awa' from here in a minute or twa."

"And these wounded?" I asked, looking round. Groaning and swearing they lay on their stretchers and in blood-stained blankets, their ghastly eyes fixed upon the roof. They had not been in when I fell asleep.

"The enemy replied to our shellin'," said Mac curtly.

"Ay, 'e replied," said a wounded man, turning on his stretcher. "'E replied. Gawd, 'e didn't 'arf send some stuff back! It was quiet enough before our blurry artillery started. They've no damned consideration for the pore infantry.... Thank Gawd, I'm out of the whole damn business.... I'll take damn good care that I..."

"The ambulance car is here," said Mac. "All who can walk, get outside."

The rain was falling heavily as I entered the Red Cross wagon, 3008 Rifleman P. MacGill, passenger on the Highway of Pain, which stretched from Loos to Victoria Station.

THE END